this human

How to *be* the person designing for other people.

D0770315

MELIS SENOVA, PhD

BIS Publishers
Building Het Sieraad
Postjesweg 1
1057 DT Amsterdam
The Netherlands
T +31 (0)20 515 02 30
bis@bispublishers.com
www.bispublishers.com

ISBN 978-90-6369-460-9

Designed by Huddle.
Illustrated by Dr Melis Senova.

For my precious son Cooper and my loving husband Cam.
You are the wind in my sails.

TABLE OF CONTENTS

FOREWORD

Because of its seminal focus on designers, this book is a unique addition to the extensive libraries of discourse concerning design and designing. It is exemplary of the work of a reflective scholar-practitioner. Dr Senova has not only reached the highest levels of academic achievement, she also has years of experience in successful professional practice. What is laid out here are her insights into the behaviour of designers-in-action as human 'beings'. Her ideas are intended to help rebalance the lopsided attention paid to the means and methods of designing in professional practice and academia. She does this by looking towards the nature and character of the designers themselves.

This is not merely a shift of attention from one end of a dichotomy to another —although in this case it is both welcome and necessary. It is an essential redirecting of focus for both education and professional purposes. This book refocuses attention on the liminal spaces in-between elements found in categories of differences, opposites, contrasts and similarities. It is also about the liminal spaces in-between uncategorical particulars—between unique people. The individual chapters in this book provide both conceptual and practical insights for working effectively with self and with others.

This shift of focus to what is happening inbetween creative thinking and effective action reveals the essence of a human-centred approach to design as spotlighted in this book. It illuminates the goings-on in the space between personal identity and externalised design processes. It does not focus on consumers, end users or customers, as is the case for many contemporary design thinking approaches. It focuses on the human being inbetween the design clients and the subsequent designed outcomes. This focus makes it possible for designers to learn how to engage head-on in self-designing through self awareness and self assessment.

Although not called out specifically by name in the book, the inbetween spaces are implied when looking at the chapters' intentions, which are quite systemic. The spaces can be envisioned as being filled in by a fulcrum for balancing contrasts, as a mediation point between interior and exterior perspectives, as a place for the integration of mindfulness and cognisance, and as a place for centering diversity.

The concepts of balance, mediation, integration and centering emerge from the rich examples, suggested exercises, clear descriptions and schemas found in each of the chapters. The implied processes of balancing between the subjective and objective, or of mediating between the inner and outer worlds of self and other, is augmented by the processes of dynamic integration which is essential for the creation of synergies and emergent qualities in designed outcomes.

The process of centering is closely related to grounding. This book speaks to the challenge of recognising and enabling the values and beliefs of the humans who are the designers, as well as the stakeholders. The author provides key advice and effective exercises for helping people to understand where

they stand and upon what they stand.

The book explores, from a variety of station points, the relationships, links and connections that bridge between people, as well as between people and their environments, particularly their social environments. As an example, empathy is introduced and explored while avoiding what psychologists call 'the near enemy' which, in contrast to empathy, is pity and superiority. These relationships are related to fixing and helping in contrast to serving the interests of others as a human-centred designer—the focus of this book.

Service is key to the role of designer. Character counts heavily in serving another's interests through one's own skills and qualities. Design that is human-centred includes not only what you bring to the table, but 'who' you bring to the table as well—character. This book helps people to become reflective and proactive in determining who shows up. It helps people understand their own personality better and to understand the challenges of developing sound design character.

HAROLD G. NELSON

Dr. Nelson is an architect, professor, author, consultant, design philosopher and former Nierenberg Distinguished Professor of Design in the School of Design at Carnegie Mellon University.

ACKNOWLEDGEMENTS

DEAR ANNIE

You believed in this book from the first time I talked about it—years ago, now. You fought back the ever-creeping commitments that threatened to pull me away from this project, never losing your calm, accommodating style... just like a ninja, as Cooper would say.

Working as we did, me in Amsterdam and you in Melbourne, it was easy to resent the size of this Earth of ours. We got there though, despite the challenges along the way (and there were plenty).

Although it's a cliché, I can't work out how else to say it: this book would not exist without you. You have been beside me the whole way. The words 'thank you' are not enough, but they are all I have. I am so very grateful for your support and belief in me.

DEAR NOLA

You jumped onto this project with your arms and heart wide open, as you always do. Thank you for reading every word and thinking about how best to express the message in the design. You have done a brilliant job.

How many thanks can one person collect in a lifetime? Here's another one to add to your collection.

DEAR KYLIE, SARAH, RACHEL, JESS, FEMKE, ABBY, LORNA AND KERRY

My reviewers, designers, organisers, editors, proofreaders, and so much more! Seriously, how many people does it take to write a book? There's a joke in there somewhere.

Kylie and Sarah, despite everything that was on your plate this year, you read every chapter, then questioned, poked and prodded my work. You made my ideas clearer and stronger.

Rachel, thank you for the original visual language of this book and for bringing your vast experience to this project. Thanks also for your friendship and support. Somehow you always know the right thing to say and do.

Jess, Abby, Femke and Kerry, thank you for jumping in willingly towards the end of this project and helping us get it finished.

Lorna, you are the very first editor I have ever worked with! Thank you for carefully editing my content and understanding and respecting what I was trying to do.

DEAR HUDDLERS (PAST AND PRESENT)

It is only through working with you for the last seven years that I have experienced and learned what I needed to write this book. You have all contributed in some way, and I hope you find traces of yourselves in these pages. Thank you all for your commitment and enthusiasm.

This book is for you. I hope you can connect with this work and that it helps you strengthen your practice.

DEAR BIONDA AND SARA FROM BIS

Thank you for believing in this project and listening to me when I was describing the intention behind it. You took me seriously when I asked for the book to be a cradle-to-cradle production. Thank you for working hard to find the materials and suppliers needed to make this book as sustainable as possible. You have been a great publisher to work with.

DEAR HAROLD AND MARTY

You have both been an inspiration to me, and you continue to support me in any way you can. Marty, you helped us when we first started Huddle. Thank you for reading my manuscript and offering your kind words.

Harold, thank you for taking the time to write the foreword. Your work continues to inspire and inform what we do at Huddle. I hope we are able to do it justice in our application.

DEAR MUM AND DAD

Thanks for making me. If you hadn't I wouldn't have written this book. It doesn't seem to matter how old I am, you are both still there holding up the pompoms and cheering me on just when I need it. You're both really good humans, and I love you.

DEAR COOPER

I'm so happy you're my son. Thanks for being such a wise, understanding and encouraging person. You did everything you could to help me focus on my book and you helped me think through some of the illustrations. This was more helpful than you know.

Thanks for bringing fun into every day and being my source of joy and happiness. I hope one day you'll read this book and be as proud of me as I am of you. I love you to the moon and back.

DEAR CAM

I could not have asked for a better person by my side. You are my partner in all dimensions of my life. Thank you for creating the space and opportunity for me to complete this project.

You picked me up when I was down and reminded me why I was writing this book. You sat with me and let me borrow your brain to help make sense of my thoughts. You reviewed my work—excited when my work was good and graciously encouraging when you thought otherwise.

As always, you were my foundation, my grounding, my source of energy and inspiration. I love you.

DEAR RHYS AND HEATH

Thank you for your encouragement and believing in me. I'm keen to hear what you think!!

WHY I *wrote* THIS BOOK

There are many great design books about design process, tools and methods. With increasing popularity of Design Thinking and human-centred design, we're seeing more material discussing aspects of this practice. One aspect missing, almost in an ironic twist, is what it takes to be the human who is doing the designing.

THIS HUMAN IS ABOUT THAT PERSON.

Within these pages I share what I know and have experienced as a human who is doing the designing. I wrote with the intention of evoking new reflections within design practitioners, opening up new perspectives and experiences of their work and helping you to make sense of it all.

In writing this book I connected with every aspect of my twenty years in human-centred design. I excavated aspects of myself and my experiences that I had devalued and buried a long time ago. The most enjoyable, and traumatic, re-connection was with my time studying the brain. I've always been fascinated by the squishy grey mass we carry around in our skulls. I had almost forgotten that I am a published neuroscientist, because it was such a long time ago. This fascination with the brain shaped my perspective on why some things in design are easy and others are hard. It taught me how we process information and where information gets processed. You'll notice a few scientific geeky references to neuroanatomy throughout—now you know why.

My PhD was in human-centred design. I was given the opportunity to live out my dream of being Charlie from *Top Gun* when I worked as a civilian contractor in the Air Operations Division of Australia's Defence Science and Technology Organisation. My PhD was concerned with situational awareness of fighter pilots, and I worked mostly with FA-18 and F-111 pilots. I learnt hard-core Human Factors, not only through my own research, but also from supporting the work of the other scientists in the Human Factors Lab. I also became a glider pilot during this time, which taught me that some-

I BELIEVE EVERYTHING IN LIFE IS AN APPRENTICESHIP FOR THE NEXT THING.

times you've just got to learn to fly the plane while you're already up there, flying.

I think this is why design and I get along. It is a way of thinking and being that requires you to work out the way while you're already heading down the path. It is action-oriented, curiosity-driven and resilient to big mistakes… if you do it well.

My time at Ford and Sumitomo taught me about the design process in its most tangible form. I worked as a design engineer on both the supplier and assembler side and observed how a studio designer thinks differently to a manufacturing engineer. Each look at exactly the same part but speak two different languages. They are concerned about completely different things. It was here that my passionate advocacy for the human in the system began. Although everyone knows it is a person who drives the car, back in those days human factors were still a relatively new thing and consideration for the person came very late in the design process. I learned how important it was to make sure human-centricity was there from the beginning.

Being a general manager within the Chief Technology Office at Telstra taught me about leadership and furthered my understanding of how large organisations work, or don't. It taught me about the powerful role technology plays in the lives of people and how enamoured we get with the technology itself, rather than thinking deeply about what it actually means for the human condition.

The culmination of these apprenticeships prepared me to establish my own strategic design firm, Huddle, with my husband. We work with large enterprises, government organisations and communities in Australia, Europe and the US. Huddle taught me how to be a graceful beginner and how to pick myself up after a hard fall while maintaining my values and principles. It taught me to fight for what I believed in and to listen with humility. It has been a vehicle for me to grow as a leader and a mentor to other leaders, and it has challenged every aspect of my identity.

It also showed me the endless generosity of people when they believe in you and what you are trying to do. I am greeted by this every day when I head into work. My wish is that, through reading this book, you will learn more about yourself, even if you're not a human-centred designer, and that learning will help you have great positive impact in the world.

HOW TO *use* THIS BOOK

This book is a bit quirky. It sits happily alongside other design books about impactful work, although its purpose is not to teach you a method of design. Those books already exist and they do a good job.

IT'S A BIT LESS PRACTICAL THAN THAT.

It also sits comfortably beside leadership books that explore mindsets and behaviours that support creative, intelligent and autonomous thinkers and doers.

IT'S A BIT MORE PRACTICAL THAN THAT.

Although this book is written with human-centred designers of all levels of experience in mind, it is not just for them. The ideas in this book can be applied to your own unique context, whether you're an engineer, a parent, a CEO, a student or the head of a nation. This book is for anyone who is interested in understanding what it takes to bring an idea into reality—one that is meaningful and impactful.

This Human helps you establish an ability to reflect, observe and master yourself so that your work is more effective and your impact longer-lasting.

This book will get you thinking, reflecting and seeing what is happening behind the scenes and inside you. I wanted to pass on the benefits of my experience and the insight I've gleaned from twenty years of observing people who do this work, and the recipients.

It is organised into seven chapters. This is not an accident. There is a very deliberate organising principle sitting behind the content in this book, but

I will leave this as a mystery for those readers who are keen to work it out. My research into how to organise this book included both modern and ancient wisdom about what makes us humans tick.

If you read *This Human* from front to back you'll discover that it starts with abstract concepts in Chapter 1 and finishes with pragmatic examples in Chapter 7. It is not linear. Each chapter stands alone, so you can start anywhere. I recommend you skim it from cover to cover before diving in though, as I do refer to and build on earlier content later in the book.

What you will discover is a book focussed entirely on you, the human doing the work, that supports the process of manifesting something in the real world. You'll be introduced to your own beliefs and recognise how they operate in the background, influencing your thinking, sense making and judgement calls. You'll become equipped with ways to uncover your beliefs, work with them and even change them.

You'll explore insights and findings and realise why knowing the difference matters at a deep level. You'll play with your own understanding of reality and discover why yours is irrelevant when you are trying to connect with a deep understanding of the people you are designing for.

You will reconnect with your imagination and curiosity. You'll uncover ways to help you expand your thinking and your perspectives so you can think big enough to withstand the inevitable whittling processes of bringing an idea into reality.

You will explore the role of communication and all the different and relevant forms it takes as you progress through the design process. You'll experiment with the different intentions that sit behind and inform your communication, and you'll connect with your own listening and that of others.

You will uncover the importance of working with people and connecting with them authentically, openly and generously. You will learn how to create the conditions for connection to occur between people, which will propel your work to a whole new level. You can't do work with great impact on your own.

YOU'LL SEE WHY BIG DREAMS ARE SO IMPORTANT IF YOU ARE GOING TO BRING IMPACTFUL WORK INTO THE WORLD.

You will understand the role of intention and its direction-giving power. You will revisit the role of free will in design and its links to energy and confidence. You will be introduced to a powerful framework that will help clarify your thoughts about why you're creating something in the first place. This will help you connect with the intention that is driving you to deliver an outcome that is important to you. You will explore the territories of resilience and grit, and find the determination to keep moving forward when constraints come at you thick and fast. We will breathe fire into the conversation about emotions and feelings and the role they play in the holistic design of human experiences. I have even dusted off my knowledge of neuroanatomy to explain why we find it hard to express our emotions.

We venture carefully into the realms of designing for the shadow self and look at why it is so important to acknowledge the duality of the human condition.

You will reconnect with judgements and see how they form and affect your understanding of perceived realities. You will uncover the importance of pleasure and desire in your work and learn how to deliberately create these conditions so you can be at your best.

We will finish with the acknowledgement that the real world is where your work will actually have impact and that to bring an idea into reality you need to move through many phases of creation that require different parts of you. You'll be shown the fundamentals of building trust through commitment cycles and the importance of taking your work to absolute completion.

Along the way, you will learn how to put these thoughts and experiences into action. I have made this book as tangible and practical as this content allows. And I know, as I have experienced it personally, that when you do the work, you'll see the results.

INSIGHT

Harnessing your insight to create new
experiences and explore new realities

1

THE FLOW OF

THE LINK BETWEEN OBSERVATIONS AND INSIGHT, AND ALL THE MODIFIERS IN-BETWEEN.

OBSERVATIONS

We use our senses to observe other people's realities.

TRIGGER

Our observations trigger beliefs we have about how the world works.

BELIEFS **INFORM**

These beliefs inform our biases (whether we realise it or not).

BIASES

IMPACT

Our biases impact our judgements about what's OK and what isn't.

JUDGEMENTS **AFFECT**

Our judgements affect how we make sense of what we are observing.

SENSE MAKING

COLOUR

These filters lead us to an explanation of an observed reality that fits into the world as we already believe it to be.

INSIGHT

INSIGHT

Insight is the capacity to gain an accurate and deep understanding of the world as it exists for another person. We all have beliefs that inform our judgements about what is right and wrong, or good and bad. These biases and beliefs filter the information we receive and can distort our interpretation of what we observe. This is completely normal. As a human-centred designer, you need to be acutely aware of your own biases and beliefs. You have to acknowledge and understand them so that you can come closer to true insight about the people you are designing for.

IT IS THEIR TRUTH THAT IS IMPORTANT, NOT YOURS.

CHAPTER 1
This chapter explores different ways of gaining insight and how to distinguish between perception and genuine insight.

EVERY
AROUN
US WAS
DESIGN

(Some meaningfully and some not.)

HING
D
ED.

IT STARTS
with AN IDEA

Insight and ideas aren't all that different. Ideas usually pop into our minds when we gain some new insight into something. And often, as we are hunting for precious insights in our research, they start as an idea: 'Perhaps this is it?'

Understanding and creation both start with the first hint of an idea or an insight. This happens so early in the creative process that you can't even communicate it to anyone else yet. It hasn't taken shape in your mind's eye—it's more of a feeling than a thought. You find yourself waving your hands around madly, but what comes out of your mouth is, 'Oh! Oh! Ahh... um.' You have no words yet.

Almost everything that has been created by humans started with the conscious realisation of an idea. Some are tangible, like houses, chairs, cars and factories. Others are intangible, like laws, customs, economies and borders.

When you are this early in the creation process, you need to protect your idea or insight. Give yourself time and space to explore it. Don't lock it down too quickly. You need to observe the idea as it takes shape, without allowing your own belief systems, biases and judgements get in the way of its evolution.

We need to be mindful about how we are being throughout all the stages of human-centred design. The way we 'be' affects everything we 'do'.

In this chapter, we look at what affects your thinking and being when you are working with insights and ideas. The intention is to provide you with a practice focussed on understanding how you operate when you are doing your work as a human-centred designer. You will get to know how your sense of self informs your work, and be mindful that what you are designing is meaningful and deliberately considered. You will learn how to ensure that you are working with the 'truth' rather than just your perceptions.

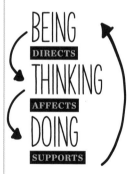

Our being directs our thinking and affects our doing. If our doing is meaningful, it supports our being.

BELIEF
and BEING

Beliefs are like operating systems. They are the framework for how we experience life. Our beliefs are given to us by our parents, our culture and our society and they become so deeply embedded that we don't even realise we have them. Some of these beliefs are about ourselves—our capabilities and limitations. Some are about the world—what is right or wrong, possible or impossible. What we are told, what we observe, learn and experience, all gets laid down as sense making pathways in our brains. Some of these neural pathways get reinforced as we hear and experience the same things again and again, and some fade away.

Beliefs protect us and allow us to function in society. They inform how we process information and draw meaning from the things we experience. But some beliefs can be toxic and damaging. These are usually the ones we've created about ourselves, perhaps because of something we experienced when we were very young. And because beliefs help us derive meaning from our experiences, they become self-reinforcing. This is a crucial point for the practice of human-centred design. If we are not aware of our beliefs and how they affect our work, we may seek evidence that builds upon what we already believe, rather than seeing the truth of someone else's reality. We have to be acutely aware of what beliefs are operating and then do our best to hold them at bay.

WHERE BELIEFS COME FROM

There are two main sources of beliefs. Some are formed from external inputs and others are formed when we decide something about ourselves.

External beliefs come from the work around you, your society, your cultural heritage, your family and your social network. They serve a very important purpose—they help you understand and navigate your life.

"OUR BELIEFS SHAPE OUR REALITY, AND OUR REALITIES SHAPE OUR BELIEFS."

Anodea Judith

One trick of external beliefs is that because they are mostly unconscious they can become outdated, especially if you are not normally exposed to different lifestyles, cultures and societal rituals. It is important that you keep your beliefs upgraded and in line with current times, and also your ever-changing self. In order for your work to be meaningful and not biased by your own prejudices, you need to be familiar with these external beliefs. You need to be aware of their ability to prevent you from connecting with real insight.

Self-created beliefs can be formed from an experience in the playground, or something your mother said to you, or just because you decided something about yourself is true. They are often a statement about what you can or can't do, or what is or isn't 'you'. Self-created beliefs can be energising and help to propel you forward, or they can limit you and hold you back. Making them conscious and being mindful of them will help you become more effective in your practice.

HOW BELIEFS LIMIT US

There is a voice inside your head that sounds remarkably like your own voice. Let's call it your inner critic. It says things to you that you would never say out loud or to anyone else.

- *You'll never be able to do this.*
- *You're not good enough to pull this off.*
- *You just want to do this so you look good in front of your friends.*
- *There's no point, it's already been done before.*

Your inner critic is the constant chatter that talks about all the things that are unlikely, wrong or imperfect about your work. You MUST NEVER listen to your inner critic when you are working with insights and ideas.

There is a time and place for your inner critic to take centre stage, like when you are critiquing your own work for robustness or making sure you are delivering on the outcomes you set out to achieve. But it is absolutely not welcome when you are trying to foster brand new thinking.

EXTERNALLY-CREATED BELIEFS

SELF-CREATED BELIEFS

BELIEF SOURCES
Beliefs come from things society tells you about right and wrong, and things you decide about yourself.

WORKING WITH BELIEFS

Uncovering your beliefs helps you
understand how they influence you.

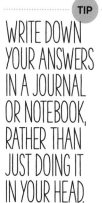

TIP

WRITE DOWN YOUR ANSWERS IN A JOURNAL OR NOTEBOOK, RATHER THAN JUST DOING IT IN YOUR HEAD.

This gives you a
useful record to refer
back to during the
various stages of your
project. It's always
interesting to see if
something shifts as
you progress through
your work.

STEP 1

UNCOVER YOUR BELIEFS

The first step is to spend time uncovering
your beliefs. This is more like excavation
than exploration. They are deep inside you,
so you need to be patient and committed
to finding them. It is a pretty straightforward process, although we often
don't include it as part of our practice
as human-centred designers. Ask yourself
these questions:

- *What do I believe about what I am
  seeing, hearing, feeling, thinking,
  saying and doing?*
- *What do I believe about the people
  I am observing?*
- *What do I believe about the project
  and its outcomes?*
- *What do I believe about how I am going
  and the quality of the work I'm doing?*
- *What do I believe about my beliefs?*

STEP 2

UNDERSTAND YOUR BELIEFS

Once you've answered the questions in
step 1, reflect on these beliefs by asking
these guiding questions:

- *Where did this belief come from?
  Did I make it up, or is it someone
  else's that I have adopted?*
- *What is the advantage of having this
  belief? How would this project run if
  I didn't hold this belief?*
- *Am I willing to change this belief?
  If so, what would I change it to?*

This activity shows you how to work with your beliefs. Working with beliefs makes you aware of what is informing your thinking.

STEP 3
CREATE NEW BELIEFS

It almost seems ridiculous to boil it down to this simple exercise. Surely beliefs are tricky and slippery and don't just change overnight?

Sometimes they do. If we work at a conscious level, we can influence them. And, slowly, they change. But first you need to give yourself permission to do it. It almost feels like you're hacking your brain.

Working only with those beliefs that are preventing you from doing your best work, write down new beliefs that are more empowering and beneficial to your work.

TIP YOU CAN START WITH THE OPPOSITE OF THE LIMITING BELIEF YOU ALREADY HAVE, BUT DON'T STOP THERE. USE YOUR IMAGINATION TO CREATE AN ENERGY-GIVING VERSION OF THE OLD BELIEF. ONE THAT EXCITES AND MOTIVATES YOU.

STEP 4
PUT NEW BELIEFS INTO ACTION

Simply working out what your beliefs are and coming up with better ones isn't enough. You need to incorporate the new belief into your daily practice as a human-centred designer. Without action and reinforcement, the new pathways in your brain won't get laid down.

The best way to do this is to share them with your colleagues. Tell them about your new beliefs. Ask them to remind you of them as your work progresses. Write them down on a sticky note and put it somewhere that you will see regularly. And when it comes up for you, put it into action.

CREATE A NEW BELIEF
Replace limiting beliefs with ones that serve you better in your work. For example, a limiting belief like 'The stakeholders are so much more senior than me', could become 'The stakeholders are people just like me, and I know a lot about my project'. Remember to put your new belief into action. If you don't act differently because of a new belief, it will shrivel up and die. Put it to work.

OWNING
your BIASES

Understanding our beliefs allows us to be aware of how these beliefs affect how we perceive the world. It exposes the biases we carry about the things we observe.

KNOW YOUR OWN BIASES

Biases can be conscious or unconscious. The key to uncovering them is knowing that you have them in the first place. We all do, and they wreak havoc when we are trying to see something for what it really is, instead of what we think it means.

> *'The process of perception is, not surprisingly, a biased one. We have loads of biases hardwired into our brains: preferences for people who are similar to us or who are in our group; wariness of those who are different; a tendency to save mental energy by using shortcuts like stereotypes to fill in the blanks about others.'—Heidi Grant Halvorson*

Your biases affect how you encounter the world. They establish what makes you feel comfortable or not, what you are fearful of or not. Sometimes in our work as human-centred designers, we find ourselves in situations where we need to connect with a reality that is far outside our own comfort zone. It might be to do with domestic violence, religion, gambling, cancer or fashion but, regardless of the topic, there is probably some preconceived bias lurking away in the background somewhere.

Biases are normal, and in our line of work it is important to pay attention to them.

> *'Accepting personal biases makes them less, not more, likely to impact others.'* —*Howard J Ross*

To experience how subtle your biases are, take the Implicit Association Test (IAT) designed by Dr Anthony Greenwald. The link can be found in the references at the end of this book.

In addition to the biases that affect your sense making and judgements on other's realities there is also confirmation bias that reinforces the beliefs you already have. Because our brains are excellent at seeing patterns in behaviour, we use these observations to reinforce our already existing beliefs or biases.

Although you may not want to accept that you have biases, they are part of human nature. The best thing you can do is acknowledge you have them and try to uncover and learn as much about them as possible. Becoming aware of your own biases also allows you to be aware of other people's. This is a fundamental skill for establishing intentional communication with them about your work.

TIP

THE FIRST STEP TO NOT LETTING YOUR BIASES AFFECT OTHERS IS TO ACCEPT YOU HAVE THEM.

OVERCOMING BIAS

Working with your bias helps you become more mindful and open when approaching your work.

This simple strategy will help you connect with your biases so you can work effectively with them.

TELL YOURSELF THE TRUTH

STEP 1
Be honest with yourself about your preferences and what is informing them.

LEARN MORE ABOUT YOURSELF

STEP 2
Explore your beliefs from Exercise 1.1 and evaluate how they might bias your thinking or your preferences in different circumstances.

LEARN MORE ABOUT OTHERS

STEP 3
Immerse yourself in contexts that make you feel uncomfortable. Learn more about people you don't understand or are afraid of.

SEEK FEEDBACK FROM PEERS

STEP 4
There's nothing like somebody else being your mirror. Ask the people you work with to comment on their perception of your preferences and thinking.

NOW TAKE A STAND

STEP 5
If you suspect the consequences of bias are going unnoticed, take a stand. Action is the only real way of changing thinking and behaviour.

Beginner's mind builds your ability to discern the way things *really are*, rather than imposing your own meaning onto other people's realities by passing them through your personal filters.

PASSING JUDGEMENT

Sometimes you'll find yourself working with material you are unfamiliar with because it lies outside your personal life experience. In situations like these we often grasp for ways to make sense of what we are discovering and, in the process, we make judgements. Our beliefs inform our biases, and our biases lead us to judgements.

To uncover insight, you need to dispel thoughts about what is right and wrong, good or bad, acceptable or unacceptable. This makes you less likely to pass judgement on what you are observing.

BECOME A BEGINNER

Our most precious ability as human-centred designers is to see things objectively and uncover deep insight. To do this with wisdom, you need to cultivate a beginner's mind. This Zen concept focuses on seeing things anew, free from the filters of your beliefs, your biases, your past experiences and your expertise. Cultivating a beginner's mind enables you to practise the discipline of cleaning out any unhelpful constructs that might get in the way of seeing things clearly.

The importance of cleaning out our brains is elegantly highlighted in this Zen story.

A professor visits a Japanese master to inquire about Zen. The master serves tea. When the visitor's cup is full, he keeps pouring. Tea spills out of the cup and onto the table.

'The cup is full!' says the professor. 'No more will go in.'

'Like this cup,' says the Zen master, 'you are full of your own opinions and speculations. How can I show you Zen unless you first empty your cup?'

When you are working with insights and ideas, you need to keep your mind open. Beginner's mind is a useful state of being to ensure that not only are you ready to know things differently, but you are also open to new possibilities that may arise from that new knowledge.

> *"In the beginner's mind, there are many possibilities, in the expert's mind, there are few."*
>
> Zen Master Shunryu Suzuki

These mindsets below, identified in collaboration with Professor Harold Nelson, can help you be a powerful and effective practitioner.

ADOPT A DIFFERENT MINDSET

There are many different mindsets that can be occupied during human-centred design, and we tend to cycle through them all.

BEGINNER'S MIND

Forever learning, seeing things anew, living in the present, not the past.

LIQUID MIND

Ability to change perspectives and positions on things.

OPEN MIND

Inviting new perspectives and beliefs, willingly augmenting your own thinking.

CREATIVE MIND

Giving yourself the permission to see that everything is up for questioning, that anything can be changed in creative ways.

DISCIPLINED MIND

Practicing mindfulness, working with beliefs and biases and practising self-awareness as a practitioner.

AWARE MIND

Having the ability to be situationally present, knowing what is happening around the topic of observation so that your thinking is not narrow.

WHOLE MIND

Being able to see the whole system, knowing the interconnectedness between the insights and ideas you are exploring or excavating.

BEING AWARE OF THE MINDSETS YOU INHABIT HELPS YOU UNDERSTAND WHICH ONES YOU NEED TO OCCUPY IN ANY GIVEN SITUATION, AND WHICH ONES YOU MAY NEED TO WORK ON.

TIP

BE CAREFUL OF CERTAINTY

One of the biggest blocks to cultivating a beginner's mind is certainty. When we are seeking insight or coming up with a new idea, we are not certain of anything. That is completely OK.

Sometimes, however, we work with people who have a lot of certainty about the direction of a project or come up with a solution very early in the process. This needs to be navigated carefully.

Certainty can be one of the greatest risks to open-mindedness. Gaining new knowledge requires us to expand our belief system but, when we are sure we already know something, new information can't get in. Certainty about your current reality translates to refusal to learn.

Certainty stems from past experience. It is informed retrospectively. When we are creating new realities, we are also creating new experiences that have no neural pathways associated with them yet. So why rely on pathways that already exist, and that come from a different time and a different context?

During the early stages of insight and idea conception, we must be willing to remain open. We must learn and learn and learn and believe that we don't really know anything about how this work may pan out. In fact, we don't even know how to talk about it yet.

Throw certainty out the window at this stage. You're going to need it later, but it's a thorn in your side right now.

BE MINDFUL OF JUDGEMENTS

Being mindful of whether you're being judgemental or being judged by others is crucial for making sense of your own work and the dynamics surrounding it.

TIP USE THIS CHECKLIST TO HELP YOU REMAIN OPEN AND EMPATHIC ABOUT THE CONTENT OF YOUR WORK AND THE PEOPLE INVOLVED.

EMPATHY

Are you aware of the other person's experience of their own reality? If not, find out.

SITUATION/ACT

Are you separating a situation or action from the personality? Be careful not to attribute your thoughts about a situation or act to the personality of the individual or group involved.

VALUES

Whose values are you using to evaluate the situation? Yours or theirs? You should be understanding their realities using their value system, not your own.

KNOWLEDGE

How much do you really know about the situation? Often, as we learn and understand more, we become less certain about our judgements.

"THE INTUITIVE MIND
IS A SACRED GIFT AND
THE RATIONAL MIND
IS A FAITHFUL SERVANT.
*We have created a
society that honours
the servant and has
forgotten the gift.*"

Albert Einstein

SENSE MAKING

We often rely too heavily on our brains to make sense of our work. This may seem like an odd thing to say ('What else am I going to use? My elbow?'), but there is a lot to be said about how we make sense of our environments and a good chunk of it isn't processed consciously.

There are many skills you need to develop as you become a masterful practitioner in human-centred design. One of them is knowing how to use your body to help make sense of what you are observing, or help you create something meaningful. You can leverage your sub-conscious in ways that your conscious mind can use.

VALUE YOUR INTUITION

I have a saying that my colleagues often hear: 'Perhaps you need to meditate with the Post-its'. What I mean is sometimes you can't push through to insight. You need to step away from your work and sit in silence and solitude for a while before your thoughts begin to crystallise and make sense to you. This gives your intuition a shot at being heard.

But walking away from work can feel like a scary waste of time, especially when you need to deliver. I remember working with an industrial designer early in my career (now an old friend). When he was under pressure and a deadline was looming, I would often see him at his desk making model cars out of paper. If this was relevant to what we were delivering in three hours I wouldn't have had cause for concern, though it often wasn't. He was doing something completely unrelated to the project, in a completely unrelated medium. He was using his hands instead of his brain. He understood the power of allowing other parts of his body to do the thinking, rather than relying on his conscious brain to do all the heavy lifting. And when he did that, the work he produced was inspirational.

As you collect information, conduct research and travel through life, you are supplying your senses with information, whether you are consciously aware of it or not. Your brain doesn't consciously note everything you perceive—it is not the only mechanism you have available for sense making. You have an entire body that helps you with this task.

Most inputs are not raised to the level of your attention at all, but they are processed regardless. *These subconscious processes are the feedback system that informs your intuition.*

Our subconscious minds should get more credit than they do. All your reading, research and the time you spend observing isn't just feeding your cortex. Your subconscious is also being exposed to the same inputs, storing information and turning it into knowledge. Relying purely on your higher cortical function for sense making employs only a small proportion of the many ways in which you process information. You need to give your subconscious time to absorb meaning so that you can connect with

it and act on it. This requires you to step away and occupy your conscious mind with something unrelated.

When seeking insight, you must learn to rely on your intuition. You need to have faith in it, and trust that it is informed by your work and is a valuable and useful repository of knowledge. You also need to build techniques and tools to allow yourself to connect with your intuition, really listen to it and make sense of what it is saying.

Often your intuition speaks to you in feelings, not words. Sometimes metaphors which might not have explicit meaning in the specific context of your exploration come to mind. Your brain needs to do the translation. It's like trying to explain a gut feeling. Learn to have faith in this process, and your process will be unique.

"We live in a world where we are taught from the start that we are thinking creatures that feel.

The truth is, we are feeling creatures that think." *Jill Bolte Taylor*

WORKING WITH YOUR SUBCONSCIOUS

When you work, all parts of your consciousness are at work. Learning to tap into and trust your intuition effectively helps you gain deeper insight. Stepping back to connect with your subconcious helps you make sense of what you're observing.

THE MORE YOU GIVE YOUR SUBCONSCIOUS TO WORK WITH, THE MORE IT WILL GIVE BACK.

REPETITION

Your subconscious mind thrives on repetition—many of your habits are essentially run by your subconscious. Using repetition to deliberately feed your subconscious brain is an important practice. It ensures you're using more than just your conscious brain to do the work.

The nature of design is that it involves a lot of iteration and repetition, but it is important to do this intentionally. Deliberately explore how your insights fit together, draw framework after framework, try different orientations, different groupings, different meanings, and get your thoughts out of your head and onto paper as often as you can.

Prototype your ideas and your insights —the more you do this, the more you'll be able to leverage your subconscious.

TALK TO YOURSELF

You do it already—we all do! This step is really just making something that you already do more deliberate. For example, when someone asks you what you discovered in your fieldwork, ask yourself, 'What was it that I found interesting in the last session?' The answer will come. It might be a series of images in the form of memories, or you might feel emotions or hear sounds. This is your subconscious answering you.

You can also do this with your work. Ask yourself, 'What am I missing?' And actually wait for a response. Notice what comes back. Or ask yourself if that new insight is actually important, and listen to the response. The most important thing is to trust this subconscious dialogue. It's your intuition trying to talk to you.

ASK YOURSELF A QUESTION, THEN BE QUIET AND WAIT FOR AN ANSWER.

(YES, WE'RE SERIOUS ABOUT THIS.)

KEEP AN INSTINCT JOURNAL

As you are working through your project, keep an instinct journal. This is where, at the end of each day, you sit with your intuition and have a chat. Write down what your gut is telling you about the work you did that day, or where your work is heading.

Make sure you don't form an attachment to these points that you write down. The purpose of this exercise is to form a practice to close off the day, and also to become fluent in communicating with your intuition. It's not an opportunity to guess at an answer, because then you become vulnerable to confirmation bias—seeking evidence for something that you've already decided is the answer.

THIS IS THE MOST IMPORTANT TOOL TO HELP YOU CONNECT WITH YOUR INTUITION ABOUT YOUR WORK. IT CAN ALSO BE INTERESTING TO READ IT BACK WHEN YOUR PROJECT IS FINISHED.

CONNECT WITH PERSONAL MEANING

We do our best creating when we know why we are creating in the first place. What do we intend to do with the energy we are expending into developing this idea? How is this aligned with our inner purpose? Seeking meaning in the work we do connects us with a sense of living a worthwhile life, beyond the immediate deliverables of the project.

Knowing why you are doing the work, and who your work is ultimately in service of, helps connect you with meaning. This meaning will provide the direction and intention of your creation as it becomes manifest in the physical world. It acts like a compass. You can come back to it again and again to make sure that you are creating with a clear purpose. Without this, it's easy to lose your way and then just stop. Connecting with meaning is your protection against such a fate.

REMAIN RELEVANT

Sense making can get tricky, especially at the early stages of your work, because everything is still so abstract. The first inkling of an idea is formless and nebulous and it's easy to get lost in your own thoughts. It's important to ensure you continue to work within the context that was set at the beginning of the project.

This doesn't mean you should focus purely on the objective you have set out to achieve. It means you need to maintain your sense of direction. If you can maintain a connection to your context, you will find things and learn from them as you go. You will probably need to change your understanding of the outcome as new insights emerge. It's OK to let new knowledge change the game—that's the power of human-centred design.

Never lose track of where you are heading. Looking aimlessly for insights is a treacherous path. Insights can be found everywhere about anything—your role is to ensure you are uncovering insights that are relevant to the emergent set of questions that are the keys to the outcome you have set out to achieve.

PAS

"I HAVE NO SPECIAL TALENTS. I AM ONLY SIONATELY CURIOUS."

Albert Einstein

FOSTER YOUR CURIOSITY

Without curiosity, we don't ask questions. Without questions, we don't uncover new knowledge and arrive at new insights. Curiosity is the energy that drives you to keep looking, keep digging and keep deepening your understanding.

There is a subtlety to this curiosity. It is one of meaningful enquiry. It seeks to gain empathy about the human context you are trying to understand. It's not about objectively reporting your findings, it's driven by something deeper, a part of you that is willing to feel what others are feeling.

Curiosity is the energy that fuels activity and leads your gaze to unexplored territory. The objective of building empathy requires you to be careful and respectful of the people under enquiry and observation. This curiosity also puts you in a learning mindset, so you are less likely to be protective of an idea or a design which is under review or testing. Seeking to learn more helps you connect with your beginner's mind, which also helps you ensure you don't have too many beliefs and biases getting in the way.

The good news is that we were all children, and children are great at being curious and learning about the world through a process of discovery and exploration. You already know how to do it.

As we become adults, we favour certainty and security and become less enthusiastic about stepping into the unknown. But if you are passionate about doing meaningful work as a human-centred designer, this is precisely what you need to do.

Make yourself a collector of life experiences, and be guided by your own values, principles and passions. The more you experience, the more you will be able to draw on these experiences when you are making sense of how other people live. A narrow set of experiences makes it more difficult to get to the truth of other people's realities.

ASKING THE RIGHT QUESTIONS

HOW MIGHT WE...?

Establish the habit of summarising your brief in one question: 'How might we...?' This becomes your guiding star for your work. It doesn't prescribe an outcome or an approach, and it certainly doesn't come close to suggesting an answer, but it does keep you pointed in the right direction. It ensures you are always on track towards a meaningful outcome.

SO WHAT IF I FOUND THIS INSIGHT?

HOW DOES THIS HELP THE PEOPLE I AM DESIGNING FOR?

IS THIS JUST AN INTERESTING CONCEPT I'VE COME UP WITH?

IS THIS RELEVANT TO THE CONTEXT OF MY ENQUIRY?

SO WHAT?

There is a very good chance that you will get very excited about your findings and insight, your ideas and concepts. You might even be a little seduced by them—a nice affliction referred to as 'solution seduction'. To test the relevance of an idea or insight, ask yourself a very simple yet blunt question: 'So what?' This forces you to think objectively about the importance and relevance of your insight or idea.

This is an art that has to be mastered—you don't want to be overly critical and allow your inner critic to shut your ideas down. Think of these questions as stress testing. Use them to make sure you aren't following a path that is unconnected with the reason you are doing the work in the first place.

GIVING YOUR CURIOSITY A WORKOUT

Make yourself a collector of life experiences. By being curious and welcoming diverse experiences, you'll be able to make better sense of your observations, and your work.

BUILD YOUR KNOWLEDGE

Seeding your brain with different types of knowledge provides you with different frames of reference to use when you are making sense of your work. My background is in biomedical engineering, I studied neurosciences and did a PhD in human-centred design. About four years ago, I decided to study Feng Shui. It was way outside my usual reading and was a completely different type of knowledge. It certainly wasn't logical and based on cause and effect—it was more abstract and mystical. This was a leap into the unknown for me. It brought richness to my interest areas and I read more widely now.

READING WIDELY AND EXPLORING NEW FRONTIERS OF KNOWLEDGE CREATES A DIVERSE REPOSITORY FOR INTERESTING WAYS TO EXPLAIN CONCEPTS AND MAKE SENSE OF THE WORLD.

USE YOUR LIFE AS A METAPHOR

Aspects of your life can be useful metaphors and experiences that will help you describe your work or to make sense of something you're exploring. When I was growing up, I was mad about tennis. At the age of 13, it began to get serious and I decided to try to become a professional tennis player. When I made this decision, my training completely changed. It was no longer just about the game, tactics and strategies, it became about endurance, focus, resilience and repetition.

I use this story to explain to leaders of organisations that when they decide to become a human-centred organisation, their training is going to change. They need to lead in different ways, make decisions based on different values and deliver on their work using different methodologies. They cannot expect to change if they keep doing things the same way.

Your life is a rich resource for sense making and storytelling—be curious about your own life and find your own examples.

YOUR LIFE IS MORE INTERESTING THAN YOU THINK. SEARCH THROUGH YOUR MEMORIES FOR METAPHORS AND STORIES.

EMBRACE AMBIGUITY

Your work will always have a high degree of ambiguity associated with it because you have chosen to work in an emergent practice. Your next step will always be informed by what you've just learnt from the step you just took. You can't plan out every single step you're going to take in human-centred design, because you learn as you go. Sometimes you have to do things you didn't anticipate.

You have also chosen to make people the core focus of your creative energies, and people are strange creatures. They change their minds, they have hidden subconscious motivations that they don't even know are running the show and they are significantly influenced by their environment. This presents an ambiguous, dynamic and complex field of enquiry.

Ambiguity is your friend and also a gift. Working in an ambiguous context gives you many opportunities to ask questions, and the more questions you ask the more you learn. And the best way to learn is by having fun. It's OK to try new things, to create new ways of asking questions, and to establish play as a robust way of seeking insight. Broaden your perspective about how to deal with ambiguity and flex your curiosity muscles while you do it.

TIP

EMBRACE AMBIGUITY AND HANG OUT WITH IT ON YOUR COUCH. THAT'S ALL.

"Most of the shadows
of this life are caused
*by our standing in
our own sunshine.*"

Ralph Waldo Emerson

LEARN *to* LET GO

If your ideas are going to live, you need to keep them light. The same goes for your insights. Insights are not very different from ideas. Being able to really see what's hidden, what's behind the observable, requires you to surrender, believe in possibility and let go of your attachment to current reality. If you don't, you'll only be seeing part of what's really there for you to explore.

ATTACHMENT TO CURRENT REALITY

Our attachment to our current reality is a sneaky thing. Often we don't realise it's happening, especially if our job is to create new realities. There is a strong impulse to keep things just the way they are. This inertia is the very thing we need to overcome early if our work is to gain any traction. Sometimes this inertia is within us, sometimes it comes from outside.

You know that feeling of hitting your head against a brick wall? When it seems that everything—the project, the organisation you work for, the people you're collaborating with—are all conspiring to make your work even more difficult? This is often a strong sign that you need to look inward and search for attachment.

No matter how delicious your idea is, there might be some aspect of it that puts at risk your understanding of how you exist in your current reality. In your current state, you understand how things work, where you fit and how you add value. All this is very important for establishing your sense of stability and wellbeing.

When an idea comes along that challenges this, our tendency is to shut it down, sometimes before we even vocalise the idea itself. If it is our own idea, we shut it down with our thoughts. 'Too risky.' 'I'll lose control.' 'I'll lose respect.' There are too many of these thoughts to list, but I'm sure they sound familiar. This is our attachment to our current reality fighting for its existence.

Take yourself away from the situation and look internally to see what you are attached to. It might be the methodology you want to use, an idea you have, or an insight you believe is too important to ignore.

These feelings will also be experienced by the people you are working with, so it's essential that this is acknowledged up front. You have to allow a safe space for people to experiment with a hypothetical new reality for themselves. It's like trying on a new pair of shoes: it's best not to walk ten kilometres in them straight away.

IF YOU ARE EXPERIENCING EXTERNAL RESISTANCE TO YOUR WORK, YOU ARE PROBABLY ATTACHED TO SOMETHING INTERNALLY.

IDENTIFYING ATTACHMENT

When you feel things are running a bit rough and you are getting a lot of resistance from your client or your colleagues, you might be attached to something. Start exploring if this is the case by asking yourself the following questions:

QUESTION 1
WHAT AM I NOT WILLING TO COMPROMISE?

We all have our own ideas about how we approach our work. Often it is this aspect of our work that gets the most resistance. People are unsure about how we are going to go about the work we do. They are not always convinced we are going to get the answers they are hoping for. Always start by asking yourself what is most important to you personally about the work. What are you not willing to compromise on? Write a list of things that come to mind.

TIP

THESE QUESTIONS CAN ALSO BE APPLIED TO YOUR CLIENT'S ATTACHMENT TO THEIR REALITY. AS YOU MASTER YOUR PRACTICE, THIS IS AN EXERCISE YOU WILL EVENTUALLY DO IN YOUR HEAD.

QUESTION 2
WHY AM I ATTACHED TO THIS?

Look through your list and cross out the outcomes—things like quality, client satisfaction and happier humans. The agreed outcomes of the work doesn't usually attract resistance. Now look at what is still on the list. For example, do you want to make a video to explain your results, or use an online cultural probe to gather information? Ask yourself why the remaining items on your list are so important to you. This will help you understand where you might be receiving resistance and why.

QUESTION 3
WHAT IS AT RISK IF I WERE TO COMPROMISE ON THIS ISSUE?

Be brutally honest with yourself about what is at risk if you let go of your attachment. Sometimes it's about getting your way, or being able to lead. Sometimes it's about worrying that if you do it another way you won't get a good result. Sometimes you just aren't willing to try something new. Think about exactly what is at risk and write it down.

QUESTION 4
DOES THIS SERVE THE OUTCOME OF THE PROJECT?

Think objectively about whether or not the thing you are attached to serves the outcome of the project. Sometimes we want to do things a certain way because we are keen to try out a new technique or we think it is the most efficient way to get what we need. However, if the people you are working with are not familiar with that approach, remaining attached to it won't serve the outcome of the project.

QUESTION 5
WHAT IS THE BEST SCENARIO IF I DO COMPROMISE?

Imagine a scenario in which you let go of your attachment and you are comfortable with that. This helps you move past your attachment and create a new situation where everyone is happy and the work is done to a high standard. Remember, people do their best work when they feel comfortable and happy with their ability to add value. If they feel as if they are being led down a path they are unsure of, you will be battling their resistance for the duration of the project.

DIFFERENCE BETWEEN FINDINGS AND INSIGHTS

Findings describe what people do; insights describe why they do it. Always seek to understand the belief and motivation that sits behind your observation.

JANE LIKES TO WATER HER GARDEN IN THE MORNING SUN. SHE DOES THIS EVERY WEEKDAY.

FINDING

OBSERVABLE AND AT THE SURFACE.

INSIGHT

ROOT OF THE OBSERVED BEHAVIOUR AND BELOW THE SURFACE.

CONNECTING WITH NATURE FIRST THING IN THE MORNING PROVIDES JANE WITH A SENSE OF PEACE BEFORE FACING THE DAY AHEAD.

BELIEF

'Being with nature is good for me.'

MOTIVATION

Sense of wellbeing and productivity.

INSIGHTS DESCRIBE THE MOTIVATIONS BEHIND HUMAN BEHAVIOUR...

There will be times when you uncover behaviour that seems unbelievable. It might be incredibly selfless, or the exact opposite. You may find yourself sitting, your mouth agape, trying to work out whether what you have uncovered can actually be a real thing.

This is a good time to talk about the difference between a finding and an insight. Too often we don't go deep enough in our enquiry. We report on our observations and describe what we have observed—how people interact with a product or service, or how they interact with each other in an organisation. These are findings. Insight describes why people behave the way they do—why they use the product or service the way they do, or why they interact with each other a certain way.

FINDINGS DESCRIBES THE BEHAVIOUR ITSELF.

INSIGHTS ARE INNOCENT UNTIL PROVEN GUILTY, AND REAL UNTIL PROVEN OTHERWISE.

It is essential not to shut down your thinking too early, whether you are uncovering insights or generating ideas. You have to cultivate the belief that anything is possible—that anything can happen and often does. This allows you to hold incredible ideas in the realm of possibility long enough for you to do something meaningful with them. We must give our insights the chance to be proven, rather than dismiss them because of a perception of what is possible or not.

When you have an idea, your mind becomes very curious about it. It says, 'Ooh! This is new!' and prods and pokes at it to see what it's made of. A new idea is not well-formed. It's too loose and ill-defined to hold up to this early interrogation very well. The result is that we talk ourselves out of this new idea, before it has even formed into a vision that can be communicated. This prodding and poking takes many forms.

IT'S TOO... [big, small, hard, easy, pretty, ugly, stupid, clever]. This interrogation is usually the first off the rank. It has a look at the newly conceived idea or insight and begins to judge its dimensions and value. It is usually run by the program that is linked to your personal self worth and is very quick to protect you from any attack to your wellbeing. It's also pretty good at influencing your decision to let the idea go. It tells you that the idea is beyond you and...

SOMEBODY'S PROBABLY ALREADY DONE IT
This is a beauty. Somebody may have already done it, but YOU haven't done it. By the very nature of you being the creator, your idea will manifest differently to anything that is already out there. We don't have one bakery that serves the world, or one clothing shop. So what if it already exists? Creation is such an emergent process that it is almost impossible to say that what you're about to create already exists! Your idea doesn't exist in the world yet, because *you* haven't created it.

To beat this early interrogative poking and prodding you have to believe that *ANYTHING* in this universe is possible. This is the fun part of the creation process. Let your thinking form in freedom. Support its formation with the fuel of your imagination.

UNLEASH YOUR IMAGINATION
Our mainstream education system is designed to create convergent thinkers. We are taught there is an absolute right and wrong. As adults, we are rewarded for quick decision-making and knowing all the answers. We value solutions, not questions, and our imagination doesn't get a look in.

It might seem odd to couple imagination with research. Traditionally, research has been associated with graphs, charts, experiments and evidence (although we all know how fond Einstein was of imagination). Remember to be imaginative at every stage of the creation process.

USING YOUR IMAGINATION

STEP 1
CREATE NEW METHODS WHEN INSIGHT HUNTING

Don't be shy about creating new methods to conduct your insight hunting. It's easy to rely on tried and true methods for observations and research, but each situation is different. Don't be afraid to borrow from other fields of research to gain inspiration about how to attack a particular research question. Don't be afraid to engage in different ways and use different tools. How will you see something new if you never look from a different perspective?

(The small print here is that you must always make sure that any new methodology you create will give you robust results that you can stand by.)

BE CREATIVE WITH YOUR METHODOLOGY, YOU MIGHT JUST CREATE THE NEXT UNIVERSAL METHOD!

STEP 2
USE PHYSICAL SPACE DELIBERATELY WHEN SYNTHESISING

Use space to help your thinking. Create different zones within your project space to think about different themes. Change the shape your body takes when you're doing work—stand up, sit down, slouch on a bean bag, bounce on a fit ball.

Introduce variety and interest into this part of your work to keep fresh thoughts flowing. Use your imagination to think of new connections between concepts, new frameworks that help you make sense, freely associate disparate concepts to see what is triggered in your mind. You can also associate different spaces with different insights. This builds spatial memory and helps you connect more deeply with your work.

USING SPACE HELPS ESTABLISH SPATIAL MEMORY. YOU CAN USE SPACE TO GET YOU INTO A PARTICULAR ZONE FOR CREATIVE THINKING.

STEP 3
GIVE YOURSELF PERMISSION TO FREELY GENERATE IDEAS

Give yourself the permission to be ridiculous in your suggestions. Use your imagination and create freely without judgement or critique. Don't feel as if you have to seem professional or sane as you go through this initial process. Bring together your insights in new and interesting ways and dig deep into why you've seen what you've seen and how you might address these insights in meaningful and creative ways. Make sure you collaborate with many different brains to help with this. More variety means more interesting ideas.

BE RIDICULOUS. GO ON. SOMETIMES THE ONLY THING STOPPING YOU IS YOU.

STEP 4
EMBRACE CONSTRAINTS— THEY MAKE YOUR WORK STRONGER

Constraints are your friend. Implementing your new design within an organisation or community is always going to involve overcoming many barriers. The only way to get around them, especially when your work is creating significant disruptions to embedded ways of working and living, is to rely on your imagination. You've got to be nimble-minded to weave in and around the constraints presented to you as you move through the process of implementation. Don't ever give up. Just keep thinking of new and creative ways to get the job done.

CONSTRAINTS ARE AN OPPORTUNITY TO GET CREATIVE. TREAT THEM LIKE YOUR IMAGINATION'S SPARRING PARTNER.

STEP 5
USE UNIQUE METHODS TO TELL YOUR STORY

Slide shows don't really cut it when you are trying to engage an audience in the human condition —especially when you want them to experience what you did as you learned about the people you have studied. Think about other forms of storytelling that will help you deliver the message you need to. Don't rely on the quick and easy method of sticking photos and text on a slide show.

WE HAVE PASSED DOWN COMPLEX STORIES ABOUT THE HUMAN CONDITION WHILE SITTING ON A ROCK AROUND A FIRE FOR CENTURIES. PERHAPS YOU SHOULD TOO.

STEP 6
REMAIN DETACHED FROM YOUR IDEAS

It's important not to get too attached to your design —they often get torn down during testing. This is actually a wonderful thing. Use your imagination to think about how you can incorporate the results. Don't assume that you need to make your original idea work. Think about the outcome you are aiming for and get creative about all the different ways you might be able to achieve it. This might trigger a completely different design.

DON'T CLING TO YOUR IDEAS! YOU NEVER KNOW WHEN A BETTER ONE MIGHT COME ALONG. HARSH, BUT TRUE.

We do our best creating when we know why we are creating in the first place.

TO
sum UP

You need to be self aware to design effectively for others. If you are not aware of your own beliefs and biases, you will also be unaware of their influence on your insights, ideas and designs. As a human-centred designer, your intention is to improve the experience of reality for people. To do this effectively, you need to be masterful at acknowledging how your own perspectives affect how you make sense of what you observe. Remind yourself that it is not your reality that is important, but the reality of those you are designing for.

NEXT...
Your insights can only make their way into reality if you can effectively visualise them, in preparation for communicating them. The next chapter explores envisioning insights.

ENVISION

Using your imagination to envision a scenario,
create impact and visualise the pathway to reality

2

THINK

TO CREATE ANYTHING OF MEANINGFUL IMPACT YOU WILL NEED TO...

TO CREATE YOUR VISION OF IMPACT SCENARIOS + A PATHWAY THROUGH

THIS WILL NEED YOUR INTUITION + IMAGINATION + CURIOSITY

TO AVOID LEGACY THINKING + SOLUTION SEDUCTION

BIG

CREATING SOMETHING NEW STARTS WITH HAVING A VISION AND BEING ABLE TO DESCRIBE IT.

After having an initial insight, you start to see how this idea might sit in a new, alternative reality, and the potential impact it could have on the world. Don't be afraid to think big. Your ideas have to be bold to survive the treacherous journey from existing purely in your mind to becoming a reality. The biggest barrier to this kind of work is your legacy thinking—the way you were taught to think during school and by society. We'll take a look under the hood and focus specifically on linear and non-linear thinking and how to avoid solution seduction.

CHAPTER 2
This chapter explores how to use your imagination to create impact scenarios that will direct your work, and how to navigate the path from idea to reality. To do this work you need imagination, curiosity and intuition, so we also explore these in a different context.

"WE PARTICIPATE IN THE FORMING OF THE FUTURE BY VIRTUE OF OUR CAPACITY TO CONCEIVE OF AND RESPOND TO NEW POSSIBILITIES, *and to bring them out of imagination and try them in actuality.*"

Rollo May

A *clear* VISION

Working with the early stages of design can be liberating and fun. This is when you are playing with thoughts and ideas in your mind, where (ideally) there are no restrictions and anything is possible. The first step towards bringing your work into the world is to give it a form in your mind. While it remains difficult to see, it will be difficult to describe. Even if your idea isn't a tangible product—it might be a system, a service, a vision for a community or an alternative model for value—you need to start giving it some shape to enable it to become a reality. Having a vision is like holding an image in your mind. Being able to formulate this vision is essential. This becomes the blueprint you use to bring it into reality. In order to manifest your idea into reality, you must first be able to visualise it in your mind's eye. You need to hold it there, build on it, change it, morph it, stretch it and learn from it. You need to keep this vision clear and updated because this vision will guide your thoughts, decisions and of course, your actions.

CREATION
follows VISION

Humans are the only species on Earth (as far as we know) who have the capacity to imagine something and then bring it into reality in a grand way. The act of bringing an idea into reality is design and creation. This includes all traditions of creation: engineering, humanities, arts, business, science and even parenthood!

WHATEVER WE THINK, WE CAN CREATE.

This also means we need to be vigilant about what we think, so that we create things we intend to and use our creative powers for good.

We are used to thinking about envisioning in the context of idea generation and creation, rather than in the context of research and working with insights. Your findings are informed by what you have observed in context of your research, analysis and synthesis. You are the best person to communicate the work. You have the deepest understanding of what you have seen and what it means.

Envisioning is the process of bringing a scenario to life. Scenarios can be a bit tricky—they can prescribe solutions, which is not what we want to do. We want to envision the outcome as the experience of a new, alternate reality, rather than the specific solutions that make up that reality. This is a subtle difference, but a very important one.

Sometimes people worry they aren't able to create images of what's possible. Some people think in images, some think in sounds. Regardless of how your mind works, we all have the innate ability to bring together ideas and describe a future outcome, solution or impact. To access this innate ability, we first need to believe we can.

Our ability to create new realities relies heavily on our ability to *visualise* them.

MAKING SPACE FOR VISIONS

For visions to take up residence in our minds they need to feel welcome. New ideas need a whimsical Mad Hatter's tea party environment, a fertile place free from critique and judgement, to give them time to incubate. Our minds are usually the complete opposite of this. They are filled with tasks to be completed, distractions to be avoided and evidence to be found.

It is your responsibility to create a safe space for new ideas. You have already explored your beliefs and biases and the role they play in affecting your capacity for insight. The concepts in the previous chapter will help you cultivate the right environment in your mind to help with your visualisation.

While the idea is still in your head and heart, you can bend the rules that govern your experienced reality. This is a precious time, so make the most of it. Spend it exclusively on visualising your idea.

Be aware that you will start bumping up against the constructs of the current world order. Use your imagination to design around constraints, egos, politics, law and societal norms.

Remember to be playful in your work. Do some drawing, buy some modelling clay or building blocks, take yourself out on an inspiration excursion. Being playful with your idea also helps break the cycle of solution seduction, so you can stop taking your idea and vision so seriously. Remember, important isn't the same as serious.

Be vigilant about the thoughts you let into your mind. Your mind's environment is analogous to the physical space where you do your best work. Guard this space vigilantly. Your mind needs to be free from clutter so that you can dream up a scenario of the positive outcome of your work—one so compelling it will continue to motivate you through the difficult stages of your work.

PREPARING YOUR MIND FOR CREATIVE THINKING

STEP 1
CREATE A RITUAL

It's not just your brain doing the work, it's all of you. Create a ritual that sets up conditions where you can be at your best. I put on music that I know helps me do my best thinking, and an aromatherapy oil diffuser to make my room smell good. These two things are triggers for the work I'm about to do. Create your own simple routine to set up your environment before you launch into your visualisation. It doesn't need to be complicated and multifaceted, in fact, the quicker and easier it is the better.

STEP 2
REMOVE CURRENT CLUTTERING THOUGHTS

Write down the thoughts that distract you before you begin and as you continue your work. This removes them from your head so you can keep focusing on the task.

STEP 3
PRIME YOUR MIND

Go through your insights, read some inspirational material to inspire yourself, start drawing or sketching some ideas that come to you immediately without thinking about them, and away you go. Work quickly and freely. You can always go back over your work and sense make later.

STEP 4
HIRE MIND BOUNCERS

Imagine you have bouncers who stop negative, critical or fear-based thoughts from entering your mind. This requires a vigilant awareness of the thoughts you're allowing into your mind and the thoughts you are channelling out. Redirect the negative thoughts to your hand and write them down. This stops them from making their way into the creative space you have just created in your mind. After a while, these destructive thoughts will stop trying to get in.

IMPACT SCENARIOS

Follow these three steps to create a robust description of an impact scenario to guide your work and allow you to create something of meaningful impact.

An impact scenario is a very straightforward tool to help you connect with the ideal outcome of your work.

As human-centred designers, we use design scenarios to describe the human context we are designing for: their challenges, events, actions and experiences. Design scenarios are often written at the activity level, as they inform the specific design of a service or product experience. An impact scenario is more abstract and has less detail.

STEP 1
STATE THE EPIC HMW QUESTION

Creating a 'how might we…?' question encapsulates the ultimate intention of your work. This is also a great way to keep your work relevant to the original context for your work.

INFORMED BY THE BRIEF.

Example: How might we create a human-centred approach to the implementation of recommendations to improve the experience of government assistance in family violence cases.

STEP 2
CONNECT WITH THE CONTEXT OF ENQUIRY

Summarise the context of your work, who you are observing and who you are actually designing for. These are often not the same, and we can get this confused sometimes.

INFORMED BY THE BRIEF AND SOME EMERGENT LEARNINGS FROM RESEARCH.

Example: The context includes all people involved in the experience of services provided by the government in assisting victim-survivors of family violence. Our work is informed by the people experiencing the services. We are designing for the people delivering the services.

ENVISION THE INTENDED OUTCOME

What is the situation or new reality you are creating for the people you are designing for? This outcome should not prescribe a solution, it should explain the experience of the successful implementation of your work. You need to go one step further and visualise what this reality will feel like for you and for those involved in the broader impact of your work. Write down or draw what this visualisation looks and feels like to you and use it as a guiding light through the project.

INFORMED BY RESEARCH AND YOUR IMAGINATION.

Example: The recommendations are implemented in a way that is true and empathic to the experience of those dealing with family violence, so that the experience of assistance and support from the government permanently improves the life of the person in need.

KEEP AN OPEN MIND

When you envision scenarios of impact that are informed by your insight and imagination, you become very familiar with your work. This can be a thorn in your side.

IT'S LIKE A FRIEND, WHO IS IN YET ANOTHER NEW ROMANTIC RELATIONSHIP, EXPLAINING TO YOU WHY THIS TIME IT'S FOREVER...

HALFWAY THROUGH THE CONVERSATION, YOU REALISE YOU AREN'T PAYING ATTENTION—YOU'VE HEARD IT ALL BEFORE.

THIS CAN ALSO HAPPEN WITH YOUR WORK.

Your familiarity with your work can sometimes prevent you from seeing new emergent patterns relating to impact.

It is essential to remain open, to continue to see things with your beginner's mind, as if it was the first time you are seeing these findings. Remain curious about what is possible and create the space for these new connections and patterns to land.

BETTER
think BIG!

IDEA MANIFESTATION
Constraints result in your idea being honed as you manifest it. Starting with something big ensures the final version of your idea still has impact.

As you take an idea from your head into reality, it starts to brush up against things. Your idea was safe and nourished in your mind but, as it takes form, other things interact with it. It is affected by opinion, constraints and current reality. Corners get chipped off, you polish the edges up, and so it continues.

The very nature of bringing an idea into reality requires it to become denser and more tangible. If you start with a small idea, it will end up smaller in real life. You may as well think big to start with, so that as you go through the process of making it happen, it still ends up at an impactful scale.

This thinking is particularly relevant to strategic and service design, as the design context for this activity is usually broad, complex and human-centred. Being human-centred introduces complexity and dynamism into the equation, which invariably plays a huge part in what is actually possible. As a practitioner interested in the deliberate and meaningful creation of realities that have a positive impact on this world, your ideas and visions need to be big. 'Big' just means what is big for you. Don't compare your idea of big with someone else's—the world needs meaningful design on all scales.

HOW TO THINK BIG

My experience as a systems engineer taught me about designing systemically. Very early in my career, I worked on both the supplier (Sumitomo) and assembler side (Ford). On the supplier side you are concerned with components (e.g. buttons), subsystems (e.g. screens) and sometimes systems (e.g. audio, air conditioning and information system modules). On the assembler side you are concerned with the systems (e.g. instrument panels) and the super-system (cars) and, in particular, the design of the interfaces between these scales of design. The systems thinking diagram on page 59 is an example of how to apply this thinking to different scales of impact.

Systems thinking is a very pragmatic tool to help you connect with the different scale of impact the outcomes of your work may have. It also helps you choose which scale of impact is appropriate for the nature of the work you are doing.

Connect initially with the immediate impact of your work. Then ask what larger-scale system this is a part of, and what impacts are possible at that level. Ask the same questions for each level of impact. As you go through this process, think creatively about the vision you have for the impact your work can contribute at each scale.

START WITH A BIG IDEA, BECAUSE AS IT GOES FROM YOUR HEAD INTO REALITY, IT WILL INEVITABLY GET SMALLER AND DENSER.

You might find you can keep going until you're talking about the planets and our cosmos, which is a great creative exercise. However, make sure the impact you visualise is one you will be able to draw a pathway to from the work you are doing now. It is important to have this grounded in plausibility—don't draw the bow too far in case you lose the link between the work you are doing today, and the scale of the impact you have visualised.

WHAT'S INSIDE MANIFESTS OUTSIDE

Creating a vision is serious business because it becomes the blueprint that guides your work. What is inside your mind—your thoughts and feelings—are what you end up creating outside yourself. It is essential to realise that the way you are thinking or feeling about something will colour the way you bring it into the world.

If you are confident your idea is going to work and it is the meaningful translation of insight into reality, it will land confidently in reality. Other people will feel your confidence and also feel confident about it, which feeds the energy cycle. If you are unsure about it, or worried it isn't going to fly with your manager or teammates, then it probably won't. It's best to work out whether this lack of confidence is something you are

doing to yourself, like a limiting belief you may have about your abilities, or whether it is a signal about the idea itself, which might mean you've missed something and need to revisit your work.

Vigilance about how you are thinking (and being) about your idea during the process of imagining how it will manifest in the world sets up what you are going to create and how you are going to create it. Neuroscientist Karl Pribram agrees: we create things because we can think of them.

Think about research as an act of observation. We can break this act of observation into two flows of information: outside-in and inside-out. The outside-in flow is observing what we see in reality and making sense of it internally. The inside-out flow is bringing forth what we've made sense of in our minds back out to the outside world so that others can benefit from what we've learnt.

As a human-centred designer, you have the knowledge, skills and tools to meaningfully create something in the world. Presumably you've chosen human-centred design because you are also passionate about the human condition and want to create better alternatives for people around the world. You can only create what you are capable of envisioning, which is why it is crucial to foster and build this ability.

OUTSIDE-IN, INSIDE-OUT
We constantly work with flows of energy, taking inspiration from the outside world, making sense of it in our minds, then bringing it to creation in the outside world.

THINKING BIG!

How to use systems thinking to increase the scale of your visualisation.

The value in this framework comes from doing the thinking that clarifies the different aspects of what you are designing (especially if it is complex) in terms of a systems hierarchy.

SUPER-SYSTEM

IMPACT GLOBALLY
Increased productivity and wellbeing across Australia results in stronger economic growth in the region.

THE MOST COMPLETE VERSION OF THE DESIGN.

SYSTEM

IMPACT ON SOCIETY
Reduced reliance on related services takes the pressure off the public service system. Decreased absenteeism results in higher productivity across the nation and improved wellbeing.

SUB-SYSTEM

IMPACT ON THE COMMUNITY
Reduced occurrence of family violence decreases the reliance on support services relating to mental and medical health, and reduces absenteeism for those affected by violence.

COMPONENT

IMPACT ON THE FAMILY
Service designed to improve experience for the whole family requiring design for victims and perpetrators. Wellbeing of family improved.

SUB-COMPONENT

THE SMALLEST COMPONENT OF THE DESIGN.

IMPACT ON AN INDIVIDUAL
Service designed to improve the experience for the individual enabling them to receive better help, more often with a more meaningful positive effect on them personally.

WORKED EXAMPLE OF THINKING BIG!
Use systems thinking to help explore different scales of impact. The number of levels is almost arbitrary as it changes depending on what is being designed. This diagram illustrates the impact on people affected by family violence.

"Not only do we construct
our perceptions of the world,
but we also go out and construct
these perceptions IN the world.
*We make tables and bicycles
and musical instruments
because we can think of them.*"

Karl Pribram

PATHWAY *to* IMPACT

A vision is only useful if you can see a pathway to the impact you envisioned. This doesn't mean seeing every single step along the way. It is about seeing a pathway from your current reality to the one you intend to create. This sets up the intention and directionality of your work.

THE STEPS, BY NECESSITY, MUST EMERGE MEANINGFULLY FROM THE CONTEXT OF YOUR ENQUIRY.

CHOOSING A DESIRABLE PATHWAY

Whether you use a desirable conversation or a desirable outcome, tethering your thinking in the desired state helps you see a way through.

SEEING IT THROUGH

When you are visualising your ideas, you are actually looking for a pathway from insight to something real in the world. The intention is to bring together many pieces of information and insight and turn them into a coherent and understandable meaningful representation.

To see the way through, you need to be able to think about all the ways that this idea can be brought to life. It might be through words, pictures, video or even sculpture. We all have different ways of bringing form to our ideas. This is an essential step in communicating your idea to others.

There are many ways to achieve an outcome, but I prefer to focus on intentions and outcomes, rather than activities.

STEP 1

WHAT CONVERSATION WOULD YOU LIKE TO HAVE ABOUT THE IMPACT OF YOUR WORK?

Think about the ideal version of this conversation you would be having when your work is a huge success, and has had the impact you are hoping for.

STEP 2

TO BE ABLE TO HAVE THIS CONVERSATION, WHAT DOES YOUR WORK NEED TO ACHIEVE?

List all the things that must come together to make it possible for you to have the conversation you have described above.

STEP 3

WHAT IS THE NEXT THING YOU NEED TO FOCUS ON TO MAKE SURE IT ALL COMES TOGETHER?

Create focus on the next reasonable action that ticks off one of the items on the list you've created above.

STEP 1

IF WE INTEND TO HAVE THIS IMPACT...

Describe the impact, or outcome you would like to achieve from successfully delivering this work. You can use the impact scenario as a way to answer this first question.

STEP 2

THESE ATTRIBUTES NEED TO BE PRESENT FOR THAT TO HAPPEN...

List all the attributes that need to come together to ensure this impact is possible. Don't try to prioritise them.

STEP 3

FOR THOSE ATTRIBUTES TO BE PRESENT, MY WORK HAS TO...

Look at the list of attributes and identify the ones your work can directly influence. Describe what your work has to do to make those attributes happen.

STEP 4

THE NEXT THING I NEED TO FOCUS ON IS...

Create focus on the next reasonable action that ticks off one of the items on the list you have created above.

WORK BACK USING DESIRABLE CONVERSATIONS

Imagine yourself in the future having a conversation about your work, which has achieved everything you hope it will. Connect with that conversation, then work back to your current reality. What needs to be in place for you to say the things you want to about your work? What do you need to focus on to make that actually happen?

WORK BACK USING DESIRABLE OUTCOMES

Another way to see the pathway through to your vision is to start with the desired outcome. Don't make this solution specific—it is about the human experience and the description of the impact scenario in this case. What needs to be present for this scenario to play out? For those things to be present, what outcome or outputs does your work need to deliver?

BY BLOCKI
OUR INTUIT
WE ARE LIM
OURSELV
TO LINEAR,
CAUSAL TH

NG
ON,
ITING
ES

INKING.

This is a very narrow viewpoint and toolkit indeed.

INTUITION, IMAGINATION *and* CURIOSITY

'I think we're way too focused on creativity. It's misguided. We should be focused on imagination... The real key is being able to imagine a new world. Once I imagine something new, then answering how to get from here to there involves steps of creativity. So I can be creative in solving today's problems, but if I can't imagine something new, then I'm stuck in the current situation...'—John Seely Brown

TRUSTING YOUR INTUITION

The role of intuition in sense-making is so important that it is worth revisiting. As you work, you are bombarding not just your conscious brain, but your subconscious brain with information. When you have spent hours immersed in a subject, asking the same questions over and over again, you inevitably develop an instinct for the subject matter. Don't ignore this instinct. Make sure you establish a practice that encourages you to incorporate its signals into your conscious thinking.

Using your intuition to help guide the envisioning of your work is essential for it to be holistic and meaningful.

THIS WAY YOU ARE UTILISING YOUR BRAIN FULL OF INTERESTING INFORMATION AND ANECDOTES–AND YOUR INTUITION WHICH IS INFORMED BY FEELING AND EXPERIENCE.

USING YOUR INTUITION TO ENVISION

Use this framework to see how different scenarios can be created using both logical thinking and intuitive thinking. Both are as valid as each other, you made them both up.

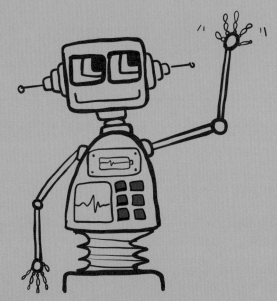

STEP 1

USE YOUR LOGICAL MIND TO CREATE AN IMPACT SCENARIO

First, try to think of the most logical, plausible, sensible and practical impact scenario of your work. Think in 'if/then' statements: if this happens, then that is possible.

Use the insight from your work to inform the scenario and keep it as real as possible. Be conscious of what this feels like.

TIP

AN IMPACT SCENARIO IS A VERY STRAIGHTFORWARD TOOL TO HELP CONNECT WITH THE IDEAL OUTCOME YOUR WORK IS IN SERVICE OF. SEE PAGE 54 FOR MORE INFORMATION.

STEP 2

USE YOUR INTUITIVE MIND TO CREATE AN IMPACT SCENARIO

Connect with what your intuition is telling you is possible. Connect with the feeling of achieving something truly unbelievable as an outcome of your work. Imagine the conversation you want to have about it in the future.

Describe this scenario. Trust that what you describe will be informed by your work, because your intuition has been informed by the same inputs your logical mind has been. It just works differently.

You might not be able to write the scenario down, you might be thinking in pictures more than words. Sketch these out as simply as you can. You just need to be able to tell the story afterwards.

As children we are taught to value rational thought over hunches. We are asked to validate or explain our hunches logically. Often this is difficult to do because it is a feeling, not a thought. This is the nature of intuition. As a result, we devalue our instincts.

Your intuition is the mechanism you have to make sense of the whole, without necessarily composing it logically from its individual pieces. Intuition is a feeling, a sensation, a knowing that can't be explained logically.

Intuition is something to be trusted. It is formed whether you like it or not, and whether you do it consciously or not. It needs to be built deliberately by connecting with it before you do something and then testing it afterwards to see if you are right. This way you are deliberately crafting your intuition, rather than allowing it to form unconsciously.

Sometimes your intuition is a trigger for further logical or analytical work that backs up your feelings. The exercises on page 67 show you how to strengthen your connection with your intuition and build trust.

IMAGINATION AS A WORKHORSE

In a society that values thinking over imagining, we overuse thinking and underuse our imagination. And although Einstein was famous for his contribution to physics, he also had some pretty important things to say about imagination.

When we focus on a thought and project into the future to think about what it might or could or should be, we are using our imagination. We use our imagination ALL THE TIME. In fact, sometimes our imaginations cause us all sorts of unnecessary grief. We craft worrying scenarios about our children being late home because a terrible event has occurred, or our boss not returning our emails because she's going to fire us. It would be much better to put our imaginations to use for good rather than evil. Our imaginations can be used to take a kernel of an idea and turn it into an inspiring vision of possibility.

"Imagination is more important than knowledge. For knowledge is limited to all we now know and understand, while imagination embraces the entire world, and all there ever will be to know and understand."

Albert Einstein

BEWARE OF WELL-WORN PATHWAYS

When you are using your imagination to envision great outcomes of your work, you need to make sure you aren't walking down a familiar pathway of imagination. The best way to avoid this is to identify what your favourite pathways are.

Our brains are fantastic pattern recognition devices. The more familiar the pattern, the quicker the brain recognises it. The quicker the brain recognises a pattern, the less your conscious mind notices it. This can be dangerous when you are visualising your own ideas, because you will have familiar patterns of imagination. These are fuelled by your world view, your perspectives and your values and they can make you passionate about certain things and not others.

UNCOVERING YOUR FAMILIAR PATHWAYS

When you are imagining an ideal scenario, it will be informed by the things you are passionate about. It's useful to know what these are so you can deliberately work outside of those topic areas and stretch your imagination.

WHAT INFORMS MY PASSION?

WHAT AM I REALLY PASSIONATE ABOUT?

Some people like to think about business solutions, others think about technology or infrastructure. Some might create scenarios around storytelling or events. It is important to know your tendencies so you can work with them, and without them.

WHERE
DO I NATURALLY
GRAVITATE?

WHAT TENDENCIES
DO I HAVE WHEN I AM
IMAGINING SCENARIOS?

ASKING THE RIGHT QUESTIONS

Knowing what type of questions you are asking brings awareness to the types of answers you will undoubtedly get. And it also works in reverse. Think about the vision you are trying to create and the sorts of answers you need to help you create it. Then ask the right questions to get the types of answers you are looking for.

A SPECIFIC TYPE OF QUESTION GIVES YOU A SPECIFIC TYPE OF ANSWER. USE THESE EXAMPLES OF QUESTION TYPES TO ASK QUESTIONS THAT...

EXPAND
- What if this exists/doesn't?
- What if this person/or that?
- What if this location/ or the other one?
- What if this happened/or that?

CONNECT
- What do these have in common?
- Is there a relationship between the elements?
- What's the nature of the relationship?
- Are there any dependencies?
- What happens when we change them?

FOCUS
- Who is this for?
- What are we here to do?
- By when?

TIP
KNOWING THE KIND OF ANSWER YOU ARE SEEKING HELPS YOU ASK THE RIGHT QUESTIONS.

"How we phrase the questions we ask ourselves determines the answers that eventually become our life." *Gary Keller*

CURIOSITY AND REALLY GREAT QUESTIONS

Curiosity opens up your mind, creating new pathways and recognising new patterns. When you are visualising, you are using the insight gained from research to feed your thoughts, feelings and intuition. You can then translate these signals into something you can communicate. If you turn on the autopilot, your ideas become stale and you lose your originality of thought.

Meaningful design and meaningful work require you to think of new and novel solutions to current challenges. To access these, you need to feed your curiosity. This also keeps your work interesting—you don't get bored with your ideas, you become curious about where this idea is going to take you and what you might find along the way.

Curiosity is your energy source. It keeps you looking, challenging the status quo and trying new things.

As you are envisioning your idea ask yourself the really big questions. What impact is possible with this idea? What type of legacy can I leave by bringing this idea to fruition? Why is this important to me personally? These questions get your creative juices flowing. They focus your thinking far beyond the details of the idea itself and more on what it might allow you to achieve for others.

Despite what we have been led to believe, questions are more important than answers. It is worth making sure the questions you ask are interesting ones, so the decisions you make about your vision have interesting and meaningful impacts.

OVERCOMING
old LEGACIES

Our education systems have made us very adept at looking for cause and effect relationships and thinking in linear, problem-to-solution paradigms. The quicker we can get to the answer, the smarter we seem and the more acknowledgement we receive. We need to step out of this paradigm of linear thinking and open our minds and our imagination to envision an alternate reality as a result of our work.

Your imagination is a unique tool. Use it to imagine things into reality.

For us to have a meaningful impact on this planet and on the beings on and within it, we need to unleash our imaginations in meaningful ways so we can dream up a better reality for all.

IT REALLY IS THAT SIMPLE, AND THAT IMPORTANT.

SOLUTION SEDUCTION

Sometimes you can fall in love with a solution to a problem. I call this 'solution seduction'. It is a phrase I coined about seven years ago and I still use it (and see it) today. It can be dangerous to converge too early on a solution, especially if you are still at the stage where you are exploring and imagining how you might visualise your work.

Here are some symptoms of solution seduction:

- *You have a fixed perspective on how this idea will come into being.*
- *You perceive other's ideas relating to your vision as criticisms and feel you need to defend your vision.*
- *You feel other people's suggestions are not as good as your idea.*
- *You think if you don't create it exactly as it appears in your mind's eye, it will be wrong.*
- *You find it really hard to compromise on any aspect of your idea.*

At the early stages of your work, having a fixed view of your vision is dangerous as it stops you from exploring other, perhaps more meaningful, pathways. You will know you have been seduced by a solution when the image you hold in your mind is fixed. When you are envisioning your ideas, these images should be fluid, they should morph and change daily as you continue to make sense of the most meaningful pathway to delivery. If your idea is fixed and you are yet to communicate it to anybody, you've converged too early and have been seduced by your own solution.

Unfortunately, the only way out of this is to break up with your idea. It doesn't need to be a complete break, you just need to come to an understanding that you need to see other ideas. When you allow yourself to experience other ideas, they bring richness and colour to your own. From here, your chances of finding a more engaging, complete and resilient scenario is heightened.

FALLING TOO EARLY FOR YOUR BEAUTIFUL VISION CAN LEAD TO HEARTBREAK LATER.

TIP

If we let our *current reality* define our *future reality...*

we'll end up creating the *same things* over and over and over again.

TO
sum UP

The work you've done to observe and gain insight will be present when you envision possible solutions. We need to trust in this process and give ourselves the permission to dream big about the impact our work can have. During the delivery process you will come across constraints you will learn to navigate, but now is the time to let your imagination, intuition and curiosity do their thing!

NEXT...
When you have a clear vision, communication becomes possible. When you are clear, they are clear. The next chapter explores intentional communication, all leading to shared understanding.

EXPRESSION

Communicate with the intention
to have a meaningful impact

EXPRESS YOURSELF

WITH

AUTHENTIC
SELF-EXPRESSION
+
INTEGRITY
AND COURAGE

TO CREATE
MEANINGFUL REALITIES

THROUGH

COMMUNICATION

TO BE EFFECTIVE MEANS BEING
EMPATHIC + GENERATIVE

WITH INTENT + CLARITY

WITH LISTENING

TO CREATE

UNDERSTANDING
INSPIRATION
FEEDBACK

HELPS YOU TO
GIVE AND RECEIVE.

CRITICISM + CRITIQUE

Your ability to express yourself is directly linked to how much impact your work has. It is important to connect with your intention to communicate and be aware that listening is also an important communication tool. Learning to give and receive criticism and critique is a vital element of self-leadership as well.

THE ABILITY TO COMMUNICATE EFFECTIVELY IS NOT A 'NICE TO HAVE'

when solving human challenges. It is a critical ability that can be learnt, practised and mastered.

CHAPTER 3
This chapter provides frameworks, tools and checklists to help you effectively communicate your ideas and findings to any audience. They will help you prepare yourself and your audience to receive essential information in the most impactful way possible.

COMMUNICATING *with* INTENT

We communicate all the time for many different reasons. This chapter focuses on the intention behind *the way* you communicate your findings, insights, ideas and concepts. It describes how you can THINK AND BE to ensure that your vision for your idea, or your knowledge about an insight, is inspiring, clear and appropriate. (Note that while the ideas in this book are being presented to you in a linear way, none of this work is actually linear, especially the topic of communication.)

Your intentions inform how you communicate with your audience. They influence everything from *what* you say, *when* and *how* you say it, to *who* you say it to. When you've spent weeks doing research and your mind is full of really interesting findings, it can be hard to know when to stop talking about them. Connecting with your intention before you create your communication approach is essential. It focuses you and stops you communicating things that aren't necessarily going to strengthen your impact.

Generally, we view communication as a stimulus–response process. I say something to you, and you respond by saying something back. When you are dealing with complex human scenarios, with the intention of creating profound and positive meaningful change, this model of communication is not sufficient. In order to become more adept at transferring the knowledge you have gained through your work, you need to look deeper into what is actually happening when you communicate. That is how you will have a long-lasting impact on those you are communicating with.

COMMUNICATION DIRECTIONS AND INTENTIONS

Use the intentional communication framework to know what you need to communicate to which people to ensure you are effective in getting the right message to the right audience.

This framework will help you think about the audience, their needs and your role in communicating with them intentionally. Knowing the intention behind your communication will inform the medium you choose, and this may differ depending on your audience.

LEADERSHIP
A group of people who provide direction and make key decisions that directly impact your work.

INFORM

The intention is to inform them so they can make decisions. They don't need to know the details of your method or your findings.

The intention is to align the collaborators with the work that needs to happen and their specific contribution. Outcomes and approach are important.

YOUR MEANINGFUL WORK

ALIGN

COLLABORATORS
Your collaborators and partners are essential to the success of your work. They provide valuable input and help you make it a reality. This group also includes the all-important 'customer' cohort.

The intention is to inspire the team to act. Connect them with a sense of purpose, direction and approach. Provide clarity around the plan of action.

INSPIRE

ACTION TEAM
A group of people that includes YOU. This team is accountable for making this work a reality in the world.

BE CONSIDERATE OF YOUR MEDIUM AND GET CREATIVE

Communication is a creative process. In this sense, the word 'creative' means the act of going from something that doesn't exist to something that does.

A concept that was once unknown becomes known through the act of communication and we can choose to be innovative and original in the way we convey it. There is more room for creativity in the communication of research findings than we allow for.

The topics we enquire about are important, so we treat them respectfully. It is possible to enjoy yourself while remaining respectful to the topic. Access your imagination, your art and your craft to present your work in a way that makes it enjoyable for your audience and you.

TIP WHEN CHOOSING THE MEDIUM AND USING YOUR CREATIVITY TO FORM YOUR COMMUNICATION, REMEMBER TO USE THE INTENTIONAL COMMUNICATION FRAMEWORK AND DESIGN WITH THE AUDIENCE IN MIND.

COMMUNICATE *to* CREATE

Communicating with people is something most of us do every day and largely take for granted. The importance of communication to your work is underestimated, especially in the realm of

MEANINGFUL WORK AND REIMAGINING REALITIES.

When you communicate, you create realities for yourself and for others. The simple act of asking someone for a glass of water creates a reality in which you can drink and relieve your thirst. The act of asking someone to leave you alone creates a reality in which you are on your own. Seeing the power of communication through this lens of reality creation gives it much more importance. This requires you to be present and accountable for what is actually being communicated and, more importantly, how it is being communicated.

AUTHENTIC SELF-EXPRESSION, INTEGRITY AND COURAGE

are fundamental to ensuring you effectively create meaningful realities through communication.

AUTHENTIC SELF-EXPRESSION

You might think that during your work, particularly the research stage, you need to provide an objective view of your findings. This is essential and true. But when it comes to the *process* of communication, you can get personal! If you communicate from your 'researcher' persona, you put up a barrier to connection. It's important to connect with your audience as a human being. An authentic expression of what you've found in your research will resonate with your audience. Your authenticity makes it easier for them to connect with you and your work.

INTEGRITY AND COURAGE

You will sometimes find yourself in the position where you need to communicate something that isn't easy to hear. This might be due to the subject matter—you may be enquiring into the treatment of women in war zones. It might be because of the impact of your findings on an individual stakeholder—you may find the target market does not want a recently launched product. Or it might be because the person you are working for is listening from a fixed mindset or viewpoint, so they perceive you as wrong or incompetent.

The trick with all of these scenarios is to retain your *integrity* while communicating what needs to be said. *You* have done the work. The knowledge is embedded within *you*. As a person committed to doing impactful work, it is vital you don't shy away from communicating the true message, regardless of the context. This takes an incredible amount of courage, but it is essential if you're passionate about making a difference in the world.

Sometimes the stakes are high. If we are to do impactful work, we need to become experts at crucial conversations. Our work as human-centred designers is not only about finding elegant solutions to complex issues, it is about being masterful communicators of our findings so they have the positive impact we intend.

COMMUNICATION FOR UNDERSTANDING

You can think of communication as an audible network that connects people with ideas and information. I like this analogy because it creates a visual image of connectivity between people who are normally not present when we think about speaking or presenting our work. This audible network connects all the people in the room. It pulses and reacts to your words, to the responses, questions and reactions (both verbal and nonverbal) that come from others in the room.

You can use this network to transmit your knowledge and the meaning behind your work. Sometimes what you say will resonate with the person listening, and sometimes it won't. Rather than thinking it is your job to transmit information, reframe your role to connect everyone in the room with your work. This changes the stance and approach you will take to deliver your message.

You will be successful in your communication when you can connect people who have different beliefs, perspectives and experiences with a single concept, so that they leave the room with a shared understanding of your work. The listening channels framework (introduced a little later) helps us get better at communicating for understanding.

OUR WORK IS ONLY AS GOOD AS THE WAY WE UNICATE IT.

One of my mantras

YOUR JOB ISN'T TO TRANSMIT, IT IS TO CONNECT.

WHEN WE TRANSMIT, WE ARE NOT MONITORING OUR OWN LISTENING OR THAT OF THE PERSON WE ARE COMMUNICATING WITH.

WHEN WE CONNECT, WE ARE CONCERNED WITH THEIR LISTENING AND WHETHER OUR WORK IS RESONATING WITH THEM.

COMMUNICATION FOR INSPIRATION

We often worry about communicating our ideas too soon. We worry that the very act of communicating our vision will have a negative impact. We worry so much that sometimes we don't communicate it at all. This is understandable. While your idea is still in your mind you can protect it. It won't be exposed to the scrutiny of others and it can remain pure and intact.

As a human-centred designer, you are in the business of bringing about positive change. This can only be done when you become adept at working with people.

You need other people to help bring your ideas into the world but to share your vision you have to communicate it. The sooner you communicate your idea and vision, the more time you have with other people to help you bring it into reality.

When it is time to communicate your work, you need to connect with why you are communicating it in the first place. What is the outcome you are hoping for?

When you communicate your idea for the first time, you are moving from the

THOUGHT REALM into the

SPEECH REALM.

You take something abstract and ethereal (thoughts and visions) and give it form, either by vocalising or by a drawing, description or slide presentation. This process of moving from something that exists only in your mind to something that can be seen, touched and interacted with is very important.

Because human-centred design is a highly iterative and self-reflective practice, every deliberate step can be seen as an intentional iteration. The first time you communicate an idea is your invitation to others to share it and start the process of making it a reality. HOW EXCITING! But it doesn't always feel like this. Sometimes it can feel as if you are about to lose something that is dear to you, or as if you are making yourself vulnerable to an attack. While both might be true for you, this step is still necessary in order for your work to become real.

There are four essential ingredients for inspiring your audience. They are not directly related to the content: they relate to how you communicate it.

THE 4Cs OF COMMUNICATION

CONVICTION

Conviction is the energy you bring to your conversations. Your passion comes from your belief in your vision and your work.

CLARITY

Clarity provides a clear sense of direction and action. You should always seek to communicate the simplest version of what you have to say.

CONNECTION

Connection enlists people into helping you create the reality you envision. A personal connection can only be formed in the presence of empathy, compassion and respect.

CONSCIENCE

Conscience is informed by your personal sense of purpose. If you feel you have deviated from your intention, you have to get back on track. Your heart, not your head, corrects your path.

?TALK ABOUT WHY

Talking about 'why' allows you to speak clearly from your conscience with conviction about your beliefs.

When communicating in order to inspire, you hope your audience will be as excited about your message as you are. In a work context, you are normally expected to provide answers rather than questions. You are expected to talk about 'what' your design is and 'how' you will actualise it. But, during these early stages of design, in the land of ideas and concepts, you often have the opportunity to talk more about 'why' you are designing—make the most of it!

People want to know the meaning behind your vision, what it is ultimately in service of and why it is important to you. Telling a story about your idea is the quickest path to engage your listeners and interest them in making your vision a reality. It creates intrigue, excitement and buy in.

"People don't
buy what you do;
they buy why you do it.
*And what you do
simply proves
what you believe.*"

Simon Sinek

During the design process, you communicate for many different reasons. One is to ask for feedback on your work, and the most challenging aspect of this is setting up conditions that enable people to do this constructively. You also have to set up the

LISTENING WITHIN YOU,

to ensure you can see the value in their critique.

You must give people permission to voice their thoughts and feelings freely, but it is also important for them to understand the kind of feedback you are asking for. Sometimes the type of critique you receive (for example, about the use of a word in a certain context) may be too detailed for the current stage of your design process. In the early stages, you are looking for broader critiques about the desirability of the idea. You could ask, 'Does this sound like something that has incorporated the customer insights in a way that will deliver something desirable?'

Is it really necessary to ask for feedback? Yes. Yes it is. If you choose not to communicate or seek feedback from your colleagues, you must seek it from the people for whom you are ultimately designing.

OTHERWISE, YOU'RE NOT DOING HUMAN-CENTRED DESIGN, YOU'RE DOING 'YOU'-CENTRED DESIGN.

CRITICISM VS CRITIQUE

Understanding the difference between criticism and critique is essential for all phases of the design process.

CRITICISM

Criticism is often subjective, non-specific and almost always negative. It might be to do with a personal preference of a colour (always a tricky area) or the way a word is used. Criticism is general and sweeping, and difficult to act on constructively. It typically focuses on the negative aspects of the design and can sometimes feel quite personal. It is up to the designer to ensure this type of feedback is taken with a grain of salt.

CRITIQUE

Critique is objective and specific. You can see how to put it into action. You can see how it might improve (or not) your idea or concept, because it aligns with the objectives of the creation, rather than coming from a personal preference. It interrogates the design or idea knowledgeably in line with the outcomes and objectives of the work, and it is not necessarily negative. The intention is to improve the idea or design.

It is very easy to become attached to an idea, design or concept. This makes it hard to accept critiques. Rather than being attached to the idea or design itself, you're better off being attached to the outcome you are ultimately in service of. There will be many pathways towards that outcome. Many different ideas and executions can still achieve the same impact. By focusing on the endgame, you can be objective in receiving the critique, and also be powerful in combatting criticism.

This framework helps you prepare yourself, your audience and environment for effective, constructive and even enjoyable critique sessions.

BLISSFUL CRITIQUE

The following steps will help you to run effective, even blissful, critique sessions.

THE PROJECT LEAD OR DESIGN OWNER. THIS IS YOU.

THE FACILITATOR.

TIP THE FACILITATOR ENSURES THE CRITIQUE RUNS TO SCHEDULE AND INTENT. THIS CAN ALSO BE YOU, BUT HAVING SOMEONE ELSE PLAY THIS ROLE WORKS REALLY WELL.

STEP 1
COHORT

Design critiques run well when everyone knows who's who and what they are there to do. Make sure you identify at least these two roles within the cohort.

STEP 2
CONTEXT

Using a connected narrative (purpose, outcomes, approach, plan), gets everyone in the room on the same page about what your project is about and, most importantly, what impact it aims to achieve.

STEP 3
CLARITY

Be very clear about the type of critique or feedback you are seeking. Set clear boundaries about what level of feedback is appropriate for what you are sharing. Give examples so your audience can level their feedback.

STEP 4
COMFORT

Welcome fresh eyes, take the pressure off yourself to say 'intelligent' things, and allow people to ask obvious questions. As long as they are relevant to the objective of your work and the request for feedback, they will be helpful.

FOR EXAMPLE: 'I DON'T LIKE THIS COLOUR' IS NOT AN EFFECTIVE CRITIQUE.

'I'M NOT SURE HOW THIS COLOUR IS GOING TO CONTRIBUTE TO THE FEELING OF EXCITEMENT FOR THE CUSTOMER' IS SEEKING CLARIFICATION OF A DESIGN DECISION WITHIN THE CONTEXT OF A CUSTOMER OUTCOME.

STEP 5
CRITIQUE

Provide space for positive and negative critique. Often negative critique comes more easily, so ask people to start with what they believe are the strengths of the design in relation to the outcomes it is in service of. Then move on to the challenges they see with the design.

STEP 6
CONCLUDE

Make sure you aren't trying to solve design problems in the critique session. This is the design team's job. Conclude the session with a list of tasks that have names attached to them. People should leave feeling as if they have contributed, with clarity about what the next actions are and who is responsible for them.

GIVING GREAT FEEDBACK

How to provide feedback that is
useful, respectful and productive.

QUESTION Always start with clarifying questions,
and make sure you establish your
understanding of the context and
intent of the design before critiquing.

Listen before speaking.
Don't talk over the designer,
listen to what they are
saying with an open mind. **LISTEN**

EXPLORE Lead the designer to explore
aspects of their own work,
but don't explore solutions
in a critique session.

CONNECT Always refer to the outcomes
and objectives of the project
when you point out strengths
and weaknesses in the design.

Provide very clear actionable commentary.
It is OK to speak from your perspective
about what makes sense to you or doesn't.
Don't confuse this perspective with that of the
customer, though. You don't represent them, even
if you happen to be a customer of the client's business. **SHARE**

The guidelines above can be provided to your critique
group to help them provide you with constructive
feedback. Invite the absolute minimum number of
people to your critique sessions. The *smaller the group
the better*. Design critiques are interesting to people,
so many more may want to come along to see the
progress. Make sure you limit this group to essential
members only.

EFFECTIVE LISTENING

Talking about your idea for the first time
requires personal courage and faith in
the people you are communicating with.
Believing in yourself and your work
puts the right kind of energy into the
room. Having faith in your audience
means believing they want you to do
a great job. Trusting them allows them

to **FEEL TRUSTED** and

attracts the right kind of listening.

Communicating effectively also
|means listening effectively and being
open to new ideas and different perspectives. Going into a communication session with a fixed expectation of how it
will go can set you up for failure. It shuts
off your listening skills and your ability
to benefit from what is said. It is a great
sign when your audience shows they are
eager for you to succeed by asking lots
of questions. The preparation you do
before conducting a session sets up the
type of listening that is required to really
'hear' what's being said.

LISTENING CHANNELS

There are various channels from which people listen and you can use them in two ways:

1. FOR INSIGHT INTO THE DIFFERENT STANCES YOU TAKE WHILE YOU ARE LISTENING.

2. FOR INSIGHT INTO WHERE OTHERS ARE LISTENING FROM.

This advanced perspective of 'listening for the listening' gives you some guidance about where they are listening from and 'how' they are listening. This allows you to shake things up a bit, or take another angle. But first, let's discover the listening channels.

CHANNEL 0: TUNED OUT

We all know how it feels to be bored out of our minds in a university lecture or by a presentation that feels like death by PowerPoint. If someone asks you a question, you only become aware of it when you hear your name. This is channel 0. From the point of view of the presenter, the audience members are checking their phones, staring out the window, picking their nails or... sleeping.

CHANNEL 1: SELF

When we embark on our own narrative about what we are hearing—'I can't believe they've brought this up again, we've already made that decision...'—we aren't really listening. When we are too busy listening to the dialogue in our own head, or practising what we are about to say next, the speaker is not being heard. Allowing them to be heard means that the message they are sharing has landed with you, regardless of your opinion of its content.

CHANNEL 2: AGREEMENT

When you want the presenter to agree with you, you often search through what they are saying to seek that agreement. Rather than listening openly to *everything* that is being said, you filter out anything that doesn't sound like agreement. This is what happens when we excitedly cut someone off mid-sentence. We think we have heard all we need to about their contribution. The danger with this channel is that we can mistake disagreement for agreement. It can result in people questioning bigger issues, like trust and influence, rather than realising this was simply a mistake in listening.

CHANNEL 3: CRITICAL

This is the most famous and valued listening channel. It is developed and used in schools and wins you accolades and commendations at work. It is the ability to listen critically to what someone is saying, look for evidence to back up their claim or test the critical direction to see if it makes sense. Critical thinking is a linear thought process. It is convergent and deductive in nature. There is a time and place for deductive thinking, though we often apply it to situations that actually require a slightly different angle, such as generative thinking.

CHANNEL 4: EMPATHIC

This listening channel has the intention to fully connect with what the presenter is saying and feeling. Empathic listening requires you to put your own motivations and drivers aside and focus on understanding what is being said. The intent is to understand the presenter's perspective and connect with their feelings. This allows you to fully appreciate what they are offering, and to incorporate your own thoughts and comments into this context. The other person feels heard, which increases the impact of your feedback. Your humility and selflessness is very satisfying for the person communicating to you. You might find they become more relaxed, and offer additional details and context that enhance your understanding. In the field of human-centred design, the ability to listen empathically to people is an essential ability.

CHANNEL 5: GENERATIVE

Generative listening almost always relies upon the listener having completely understood what is said. Understanding context and having empathy for the presenter allows the listener to enter a mode of co-creating with the communicator. When someone understands your idea, whether they agree with it or not, they are able to engage in a dialogue that is almost always generative. The trick is to also listen in a way that enables you to see their contribution as generative rather than aggressive or critical.

Because they have empathy for your perspective, they are able to build upon your idea in a way that allays their concerns. Rather than criticising your idea, they work with you to improve it. This is the space you should aim to create whenever you communicate an idea for the first time.

The following framework offers questions you can ask yourself to gauge which listening channel you are using. This is a very helpful practice, as it creates a sense of awareness about whether or not you are listening from the right place. Being aware of your listening helps you connect with your audience.

CHOOSING A LISTENING CHANNEL
We can occupy any of these channels and move between them at any time. The trick is to know you're doing it, and to realise which channel you are listening from. Then to ensure it's the right one!

TUNING INTO YOUR LISTENING

TUNED OUT

SELF DISPLACEMENT
NOT PRESENT

SELF

JUDGEMENTAL
LISTENING TO SELF

AGREEMENT

FAMILIAR
LISTENING FOR SIMILARITY

CHANNEL 0	CHANNEL 1	CHANNEL 2
Am I actually listening?	Am I just waiting for them to stop talking so I can say my important bit?	Am I listening for what is similar to what I already know, or am I focused on whether or not they agree with what I've just said?
Would I be able to answer a question if someone asked me one right now?	Am I practising what I'm about to say next, instead of listening intently to what is being said now?	Am I looking for allies in this conversation, so I know who to direct my next comment to?

TO CHECK YOUR LISTENING, ASK YOURSELF

USE THESE LISTENING CHANNELS TO HELP YOU IDENTIFY WHICH CHANNEL YOUR LISTENING IS SET TO.

A way to think about the different types of listening we experience in our work. This framework was developed in collaboration with Dr Harold Nelson.

CRITICAL

FACTUAL
LISTENING FOR EVIDENCE

CHANNEL 3

Am I listening for proof that what they are saying is right?

Am I looking for evidence to back up their work?

EMPATHIC

CONNECTED
LISTENING FROM THE SPEAKER'S PERSPECTIVE

CHANNEL 4

Am I listening from a place that has no other motive but to connect with their perspective?

Do I understand what it feels like to have that perspective?

GENERATIVE

INSIGHT
LISTENING FROM POSSIBILITY

CHANNEL 5

Am I using my empathy and insight into their context and motivation to help achieve the best outcome?

Have I taken a position of possibility, to ensure that we are able to generate a meaningful alternative?

ESSENTIAL LISTENING CHANNELS FOR INTENTIONAL COMMUNICATION AND HUMAN-CENTRED DESIGN.

RESONANCE

A scientific perspective of verbal communication is that, as we speak, audible symbols carry meaning. These *energetic emissions* travel from you, through the audible network in the group, and arrive at the next person. This person will either be open to receiving that symbol or not. If they are open, it has the opportunity to resonate with their energy. If they are not, the opportunity for resonance is not there, and there may be a greater probability of dissonance.

Thinking of your role as communicator as being the person responsible for

ACHIEVING RESONANCE

with your audience allows you to become more aware of their listening.

It is useful to know which listening channel your audience is using. This gives you insight into what frequency you need to transmit at. If your audience is listening to you from a critical channel then you need to communicate about the practical, pragmatic evidence base of your work.

Knowing when your thoughts and ideas are resonating with your audience requires you to be interested and engaged with everyone you are communicating with (as long as the group is small, of course). There are cues in the words they choose, the way they hold their body and the depth of their questioning. The following framework gives you tips on how to assess your audience's listening.

TALK LESS, LISTEN MORE

When you communicate your work, you can get very excited. You're eager to make sure everyone knows all the tiny details about what you've discovered. This can lead you into a trap, though. You might find yourself excitedly talking 'at' the audience, rather than connecting 'with' them.

Another downfall is that your ears |turn off. You become momentarily deaf to what is actually going on in the room, and you miss the subtle cues coming from your audience. In this moment, you are completely absorbed in your own world.

It is hard to fight the urge to go all in, both feet first, to describe everything in totality. That's essentially what you are there to do. You're the one with the knowledge, not your audience. But listening is just as important as talking. If you get too carried away you won't get other people's perspectives on your work, because they won't have the opportunity to ask questions.

For people who are insecure about their work, talking is a great strategy to avoid questions. If that's why you're talking, there's probably a more important issue you need to address, and it's usually to do with whether you feel confident and proud of your work. If you don't, you should really find out why.

YOU CANNOT CONNECT PEOPLE WITH YOUR KNOWLEDGE IF YOU AREN'T IN THEIR WORLD.

LISTENING TO LISTENING

TUNED OUT   SELF   AGREEMENT

CHANNEL 0	CHANNEL 1	CHANNEL 2

WHAT THEY DO

Ask you to repeat your question, or jump when you address them, or fall sleep.

Cut off your sentences before you've finished. Reaffirm a point that is irrelevant to what you've said. Answer different questions to the ones asked.

Only respond to part of what you've said—the part that supports their point of view —and ignore the rest. Reframe what you've shared in support of their agenda (not a bad thing if their agenda is in line with the purpose of your work).

HOW YOU MIGHT FEEL

DISEMPOWERED   FRUSTRATED   INCOMPLETE

TIP TUNE INTO YOUR AUDIENCE'S LISTENING SO YOU CAN CHANGE THE WAY YOU ARE COMMUNICATING WITH THEM.

CRITICAL

CHANNEL 3

Ask for quantifiable indicators as evidence that your work is sound. Ask for what they are actually going to get, or what is the tangible thing at the end of this? Look for the fact base and seek traceability.

EMPATHIC

CHANNEL 4

Ask insightful questions about your work. Relate your work to their personal context. Work with a metaphor you've used and share their perspective within it.

GENERATIVE

CHANNEL 5

Ask questions that further your thinking. Make suggestions about interpretations of your work, or applications of your design.

TIRED

BUT MORE LIKE A GOOD WORK OUT.

CONNECTED, UNDERSTOOD

EXCITED, SUPPORTED

For your work to have impact you need to express yourself.

TO
sum UP

Communication isn't a one-way street. Your ability to make an impact relies heavily on your ability to effectively communicate your ideas, thoughts and perspectives to different audiences. The intention that informs the content of your communication should also inform the words you choose, the medium you use and the audience you select. Being clear about why you are communicating and what outcome you are hoping for will help you make these decisions deliberately and effectively.

Listening skills set good communicators apart. Mastering your ability to tune into the listening of others in the room lets you tailor your communication style to make sure your message is heard and understood. Being mindful of your own listening also goes a long way towards ensuring your work has impact.

NEXT...
Solving the world's trickiest challenges cannot be achieved on your own. In the next chapter we explore how you can create heartfelt connections with other people.

CONNECTION

Making human connections
is the heart and soul of your work

HEART

DESIGNING FOR MEANINGFUL IMPACT REQUIRES MORE THAN YOUR INTELLECT, IT REQUIRES YOUR...

EVERYTHING WE DO IS ABOUT CONNECTING WITH PEOPLE.

One way or another, our work is informed by people, created by people, or in service of people. But our work is very task-oriented. We move from task to task, meeting to meeting and workshop to workshop. We don't pay enough attention to who is actually in the room, on the phone or on the screen. We tend to be so focused on the job at hand that we forget to establish a connection with the people we are working with and for.

CHAPTER 4
This chapter focuses purely on the importance of heartfelt human connection, why it is important and how to create it. *If you only take away one idea from this book, let it be this.*

IT'S ALL *about* PEOPLE

You may think it's hard to build human connection in a work context, or that it will get in the way of doing your work. It is perfectly possible to do good work by focusing on what needs to be done and delivering to the right level of quality, on time and within budget. Absolutely. No doubt about it. But the experience of getting there can either be inspiring and fulfilling or draining and empty. Paying attention to the people involved in your work can shift it from being good to brilliant. And, in my view, that's essential for anyone who is interested in being excellent at designing for people.

CONNECTION INCREASES HAPPINESS

When we build heartfelt connections with the people we work with, and those whom our work is ultimately in service of (usually the customers), we feel better about what we are working on, and ultimately we feel better about ourselves and the contribution we are making through our work.

Love is not discussed much in the context of work, but there is such a thing as

COMPANIONATE LOVE.

In a recent article from Wharton on companionate love they define it as the care between colleagues who are together day in and day out, who are mindful of each other's feelings, show compassion when things don't go as planned, and support each other in any way they can.

According to a recent *Harvard Business Review* article, the presence of this connection increases satisfaction and team work, reduces absenteeism and improves client outcomes.

CONNECTION BOOSTS CREATIVITY

Work can be isolating, especially when you are in the middle of making sense of an immense amount of data. Being diligent about keeping other people involved in your work gives you access to their knowledge, their perspectives and their ideas. This feeds your creativity and strengthens your sense making. Building real human connections with people you work with makes the work easier and better.

CONNECTION INCREASES YOUR INFLUENCE

Your work is only as impactful as the distance your relationships extend. The best way to have impact is to have more connections and more friends.

PEOPLE LIKE TO WORK WITH PEOPLE THEY LIKE.

Connecting with people and forming a network of genuine relationships increases the likelihood that your work will have a greater impact.

CONNECTION CREATES OPPORTUNITIES

Knowing people and having genuine connections with them lets you give them opportunities they wouldn't have otherwise. And it works both ways. Human connection allows for the propagation of opportunities and impact in emergent, creative and synchronous ways.

THEY ARE PEOPLE TOO
We often forget that we are working with people. And we forget that as human-centred designers, we are designers who design for people.

GENUINE *human* CONNECTION

There is a lot of talk about the seven steps to this, the eight steps to that, and a single step that will lead to financial freedom for life! Human connection can't be built from following a series of steps. However, it can be built through your own awareness of yourself, your actions and thinking, and your openness to inviting connection in.

Genuine connections occur when you are open and inviting to them. For a lucky few, this comes naturally, and for a human-centred designer that is a huge bonus. For the rest of us, especially in our distracted current realities, it takes a little practice.

GENUINE CONNECTIONS

The following ideas are designed for you to contemplate, apply and learn from. They are not steps, they have no order, they are simply for you to consider, explore and experiment with.

BE AUTHENTIC

Building heartfelt connection requires you to share aspects of yourself. This may require you to be vulnerable. We often have a facade or persona that we bring to work, because work environments can be competitive and combative. If you try to connect with people while you are being disingenuous, your connection will only be as deep as your facade.

Sometimes people are afraid to be authentic, even in encouraging environments. It takes courage to share aspects of yourself. But when you begin to share, others around you do too, and you ultimately create more meaningful relationships.

INVITE RANDOMNESS

Relax your perceptions about who you should be friends with. Be open to random connections and experiences. You might need to be a little more open than usual, a little more curious than usual and a little more adventurous than usual. For people who are interested in understanding the human condition, inviting in the unexpected is a powerful way to uncover your 'unknown unknowns'.

ACCEPT PEOPLE

Chapter 1 discussed beliefs and biases and their impact on our sense making. This is also true of building genuine connections with people. Be very vigilant about your expectations of people's behaviour, what they are capable of and how they will work with you. Be discerning about the people you build strong connections with. Acceptance doesn't mean compromising your own values and standards. It is crucial to know yourself for you to be successful at building genuine connections with others.

EXPRESS YOUR PASSION

Allow people to see what makes you tick, what really drives you. This might be directly related to the work you're doing, or it might not. It might be something completely random and obtuse. Let people see your passion and allow them to be moved by what moves you. Sharing your passions encourages others to share theirs. And sharing stories about the things that are important to us creates connections that go beyond the task at hand.

TIP

TAKE NOTE, NOT ONLY ARE THESE IDEAS APPLICABLE TO YOUR WORK, THEY ARE APPLICABLE TO YOUR WHOLE LIFE.

CONNECT TO CONNECT

Connecting with someone should never have an ulterior motive. You should be fully present, listening and attentive to what they are saying and what they need. Your only motive should be how you can be of service to them. Building connections based on a mutual willingness to support and enable another person creates the perfect conditions for collaboration and great work to emerge.

CULTIVATE IMPORTANT RELATIONSHIPS

Human connections need nourishment and attention. They are like the synapses in your brain. If you don't keep reinforcing them, they will wither away. Know the people in your life who are really important to you and make sure you cultivate those connections.

"A connection is the energy that exists between two people when they feel seen, heard, and valued; when they can give and receive without judgement; and when they derive sustenance and strength from the relationship." *Brené Brown*

"Human freedom involves our capacity to *pause* between the stimulus and response and, *in that pause,* to choose the one response toward which we wish to throw our weight.

The capacity to create ourselves, based upon this freedom, is inseparable from consciousness or self-awareness." *Rollo May*

IN SERVICE *of* OTHERS

BEING IN SERVICE IS...

- Genuinely caring about the context of others you work with.
- Understanding the needs and desires of those you work and collaborate with.
- Creating scenarios that improve the context of those you work with.

IT IS NOT...

- ONLY caring about their context and ignoring your own.
- Forgoing your own needs to deliver on theirs.
- Making things more difficult for yourself while improving conditions for others.

I have seen human-centred designers work brilliantly with customers by being open, patient, observant and empathic. They genuinely try to understand their customers' needs, frustrations and delights and are able to apply their design skills to improve their customers' experience. And I have seen those same designers walk into a client meeting and not apply any of these skills to that context.

Everything you do as a human-centred designer should employ your skills in service of the people you are working with or for. To be very clear, I do NOT mean taking a subservient stance. Nor does it mean letting go of what you need or are trying to achieve. It means being genuinely interested in understanding the context of the other person, so you can design an approach together. This is where your creative problem-solving skills come in.

To be powerfully in service of other people, you need to be powerfully connected with yourself, your work and the outcomes you are working towards. This can be challenging. It requires effort and creativity to find the pathway to making those outcomes a reality, rather than opting for trade-offs.

Walking into a business meeting does not mean that you cease to care about people. They are people too. You can apply everything you know about the human condition to improve how you can be in service of those you are meeting with.

- *What are their concerns?*
- *What problems are they trying to solve?*
- *What is their desired outcome and how can you help them get there?*
- *What do you need from the meeting?*
- *How can you connect with them in a way that is empathic to their context, and still achieve what you need?*

Sometimes we assume our roles and forget to be people. We are people first and we can only create genuine connection with other people if we remain human. This also goes for the people you are meeting with. They may have a title like Group CEO of the World's Biggest Company but they are still people, and you are the person in the room who knows how to understand their needs and desires and design a way to fulfil them. Always remember your superpower.

BE A PERSON, NOT YOUR ROLE.

PREPARING TO CREATE AND BUILD HUMAN CONNECTIONS

Here are some simple questions to ask before you design a workshop, or any engagement, to ensure you continue to build connection between you, your work and the people involved with your work.

QUESTION 1
WHO IS GOING TO BE THERE?

This can be harder than it sounds. I am sure you've been in a situation where you've planned a workshop for ten people but ten more turn up at the last minute. This works in two directions, knowing who you actually need in the workshop and being really clear about that, and knowing who is actually going to be present.

Knowing this allows you to answer the rest of the questions. Without it, you'll have unnecessary challenges to work through.

QUESTION 2
WHAT IS THEIR CONTEXT?

Clients often have many other things on their plate in addition to your project. Understanding their situation helps you design a workshop that is empathic to their context. Often we design the workshop from our perspective: what information do we need and what is the best way to get it? This is not good enough. We need to design from a human-centred perspective.

See what I did there? *Everything* we do needs to be human-centred. For example, if your client is in the middle of a restructure and has to reapply for their job, they might not be in the mood to participate in a new technique requiring improvisation and acting as a way to explore desired experiences in their current roles. A more considerate approach would be more appropriate.

QUESTION 3
WHERE ARE THEY LISTENING FROM?

The framework of listening channels discussed in Chapter 3 is a good tool to help you understand how other people are listening, but this question is about a more general listening. Are they a supporter of this way of working or not? Are they happy with the project or not? Do they believe that you are helping them or hindering them? Every interaction you have with someone can build and strengthen a connection or weaken it. Being considered and mindful in every interaction helps you create the right conditions to foster connections.

QUESTION 4
WHAT ARE THEIR CONCERNS AND OBJECTIVES?

You have a job to do, and you need to get information and insight from your work, but you should also have an awareness of other people's concerns and objectives. This will help you work out how your workshop can help them achieve those things. This attention to their concerns and objectives (whether they are directly related to your work or not) will demonstrate that you are a genuine and helpful person, without compromising the quality of your own work.

QUESTION 5
WHAT IS THEIR COMFORT LEVEL?

Some people will be very comfortable with the methods and tools involved in human-centred design and others won't be. Knowing their comfort level will help you design an interaction that they are comfortable with, while still introducing a new way of working. Don't feel that you need to completely alter your way of working to make your collaborators or clients feel comfortable. Part of the reason you are there is to introduce new thinking and new ways of working. However, you do need to know how far to stretch the rubber band. If you go too far, it will snap and you will lose them. Once you've lost a connection, it's really hard to get it back. It's better to do everything you can to avoid losing it in the first place.

HEARTFELT DESIGN

When you design from your heart, you build genuine connections between yourself, the people you're working with and your work. Designing for meaningful impact requires more than your intellect, it requires your heart. It requires your ability to understand, to see clearly, to communicate well, to have strong will and motivation, to navigate a broad range of emotions and to be present and grounded in the moment. That which is created from your heart will be strong and resilient and stand the test of time.

When you design from your heart, you have a deeper commitment to the outcome than just getting through a process. When you truly care about what happens with your work, you bring a different energy to it. There is an intensity and clarity that inspires people and makes it easier and more fulfilling to work with you.

Allowing yourself to care about the outcomes of your work can be tough in an impersonal environment. Unfortunately, this is often the case for many work environments. It is really difficult to do meaningful work when you are just moving through the steps in a design process and ticking boxes. But times are changing. More and more people are defiantly following their hearts and their passions. You can have a positive impact and also enjoy the process.

> **TIP**
> WHEN YOU ARE DISCONNECTED FROM WHAT YOU ARE WORKING ON, YOUR HEART IS JUST NOT IN IT.

DESIGNING FROM YOUR HEART

How do you know when you are designing with your heart and when you're not? It is really very simple.

KNOW WHAT YOU'RE GOOD AT

What do people ask you for most often? What do you know you can do really well?

KNOW WHERE THIS EXISTS IN YOUR WORK

Look at your work and see where aspects of your passions already exist and where there are gaps. Think about how you might bring more of your passions into your work.

KNOW WHAT YOU CARE ABOUT

If you are drawn to meaningful design, you won't need to look very far to uncover what you really care about. Write down a description of them, and try to understand why you care so much about them.

MAKE SPACE

Our schedules can be so crammed with commitments there isn't any room to do what we love. Doing what you love occupies space and time, so it is up to you to ensure you create space for that in your schedule. Block out time for yourself, without deciding beforehand what you are going to do with it.

TIP

WHEN YOU CARE ABOUT WHAT YOU ARE DOING AND FEEL PASSIONATE ABOUT IT, YOU ARE DESIGNING FROM YOUR HEART.

KNOW WHEN YOU LOSE TRACK OF TIME

Think about a time when you were so deeply immersed in your work that you lost track of time. Those occasions when you entered a state of flow and time just disappeared. What were you doing? Make a list of these activities and look for commonalities in those experiences.

KNOW WHAT YOU LOVE

Think back to when you were a kid. Remember all the things you loved doing? What are they? The things that brought you joy then will probably still bring you joy now. What are the things you do when you're not on project? Write a list.

Impactful design is not just an intellectual activity, it is an activity that requires all of you.

TO
sum UP

When you care about what you are creating, you bring an energy and magnetism to it. This charismatic power draws people to you and your ideas. It encourages them to help you create the impact they also believe in. To connect genuinely, you need to *be* genuine. This requires vulnerability, courage, and compassion for yourself and others. Heartfelt connections lead to heartfelt work. With these connections anything is possible.

NEXT...
The next chapter explores the energy that you need to fuel your creative process. It comes from within you: it is your intention and your free will.

INTENTION

Acting with intention in order
to create meaningful work

5

INNER AUTHORITY) IS REQUIRED FOR...

SENSE OF PURPOSE) PROVIDES CLARITY TO...

FREE WILL + INTENTION

PROVIDES YOU WITH

GIVES DIRECTION TO

ENERGY

TO DO IMPACTFUL WORK YOU NEED...

Creating work of impact takes energy and as practitioners we need to learn how to manage and monitor our energy. Having clarity about why you do what you do, understanding the direction you're heading in, being resilient and having a sense of authority over your work are great starting points for accessing sources of energy.

CHAPTER 5
This chapter focuses on the role your free will, self-confidence, clarity of purpose and intention plays on your ability to work through the tough challenges people face today.

A *clear* INTENTION

As an idea progresses, we arrive at the point of 'doing'. We have to actually create the thing we have envisioned and communicated and bring it into reality. This takes energy and personal power. It takes a commitment to follow through on what you've said you will do.

Human-centred design that seeks meaningful impact requires a very strong will and the ability to keep working through challenges, which will come thick and fast as the work starts to become reality. As other people start interacting with your work, their critique and feedback can be quite direct and specific. Sometimes this might feel personal. There will be times when seemingly insurmountable constraints like regulations, laws, cultural norms and even Mother Nature herself keep stacking up.

This is precisely the time to cultivate your inner strength and keep going, no matter what. The word I use when I'm asked to describe an essential quality in designers is 'grit'. Grit is a combination of resilience, determination, humility, persistence and a great attitude.

When we are doing meaningful work, changing the super-systems that organise our society, we are going to experience resistance. Not the type of resistance that says, 'I'm not sure we can afford to implement that with all those features', but the type that says, 'We'd be crazy to go ahead with this idea—it means everything has to change, including the way we run this entire organisation, and there's no-one on the planet who knows how to run an organisation with this new value system'.

The people in the systems you are changing want to protect the status quo, so they will resist change at first. When you are actually making a difference, you alter the reality of people with influence. You will need clear intention and buckets of energy, will and confidence.

As your design becomes more tangible, so do the constraints. Reality is like your honing board, or a whetstone that shaves little bits off your idea. This can be challenging. Staying connected to why you are designing and your intention will give you the clarity and direction you need to navigate these challenges. A reason that is bigger than yourself is a source of energy that drives you over any hurdle.

This energy is a creative energy. Your job is to harness it and direct it.

THIS DIRECTION COMES FROM INTENTION AND THE ENERGY IS YOUR OWN FREE WILL.

"LIFE SHRINKS OR EXPANDS IN PROPORTION TO ONE'S COURAGE."

Anaïs Nin

PURPOSE *and* INTENTION

You must remain connected with the intention of your work through all its stages. What are you aiming to achieve and enable? This is different from purpose. Purpose is something you continually seek. It is your source of motivation, not something you attain. Intention brings focus to your purpose and helps connect you with the outcomes associated with your chosen way to manifest your vision.

Purpose provides you with the motivation to get up in the morning and get excited about your life. An intention is very focused on the work you are doing and the outcomes and impact it will enable. Remaining connected to your intention provides a constant source of direction and clarity and can guide your synthesis, your design and your interactions.

This example of purpose and intention from my firm shows how they motivate and direct us in our work.

OUR PURPOSE IS TO DO MEANINGFUL WORK AND POSITIVELY AFFECT HUMANITY.

Our intention is to partner with large organisations and help change their value systems to drive more holistic decision-making. We intend to alter what it means to be in business from profit making to positive impact.

An example of purpose and intention in the context of your work might be:

MY PURPOSE IS TO DO WORK THAT ADVOCATES FOR PEOPLE IN ANY SYSTEM TO IMPROVE THEIR EXPERIENCE OF REALITY.

My intention is to create a way for the government to deliberately and meaningfully design better ways of protecting people who are dealing with displacement.

CONNECTING TO INTENTION

For meaning to be created we need a clear pathway to guide it, otherwise we might see nonsensical patterns and build very convincing cases around them. Because our form of work is often emergent and not guided by numbers, we need to rely on our skills of observation, recording and sense making.

It is particularly important to connect with the intention of your work during research and synthesis. You need to give your thinking an orientation so your sense making remains relevant to your design context. This doesn't mean you analyse towards a certain objective—that would defeat the purpose of emergent learning and insight. Instead, reconnect with why you are doing the research in the first place. What outcome does this research seek to inform? This provides you with direction in your search and excavation.

There is a trap, however. You don't want the intention to be so clearly defined you end up finding evidence for a solution that has already been prescribed. Unfortunately this happens sometimes. You need to have a clear intention to guide your sense making, but without being so specific that you miss things that could take your findings in a more meaningful direction.

As your work progresses, you will probably learn something that changes your intention. This is OK as long as there is a good reason for it, and you are still meeting the needs of the people you are helping in the first place.

INTEGRATION AND TRANSFORMATION

When you are sense making, what you are actually doing is integrating and transforming data. Sense making doesn't just occur at the early research phases of human-centred design, it happens throughout your work and has many different inputs. You integrate the data into patterns to tell a more coherent story about what you've observed in the research and then you transform that data into information and, eventually, you turn your findings into insight.

THIS TAKES ENERGY.

When you are in the throes of synthesis, you can feel drained and fatigued by the end of the day, even if you spent most of it staring at a wall of sticky notes. The amount of connecting, discarding, rearranging, challenging, remembering, deciphering and mental high-fiving that your brain does is incomprehensible.

Having a clear *intention* is energy giving.

Integration happens on multiple levels. Not only externally, turning findings into insight, but also internally. In fact, this is an essential skill to develop if you want to become great at this work. I don't mind if people make mistakes. In fact, I encourage people to make more interesting mistakes. The caveat is they also need to be rapid and complete integrators. They learn from their mistakes and they integrate that knowledge internally as wisdom. This ensures the same mistakes don't keep happening. We can learn from making interesting mistakes.

TIP THE INTEGRATION OF DATA INTO INSIGHT TAKES ENERGY. HAVING A CLEAR INTENTION HELPS PROVIDE DIRECTION TO THE PROCESS.

EXERCISE 5.1

TRANSFORMATION OF DATA TO INSIGHT

RANDOM CAPTURE
Data is disparate and unrelated.

GROUPED
Richer information gained by understanding shared contexts.

FINDINGS
Gain knowledge by understanding interelatedness and the relationship between observations.

INSIGHT
Relative importance and priorities of findings leads to insight.

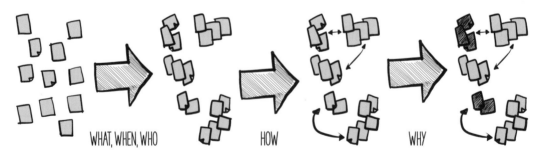

WHAT, WHEN, WHO

+ CONTEXT
Understand similarity between concepts.

HOW

+ MEANING
Understand relationships between concepts.

WHY

+ MOTIVATION
Understand relative importance of concepts.

SETTING A CLEAR INTENTION FOR YOUR WORK

This is an anatomy of a good intention, but it won't fit every context. You will have to adjust it as necessary; however, it does give you a place to start.

A good intention statement keeps you focussed on who you are helping and why.

⌒ WE INTEND TO... ⌒

	EXAMPLE 1	EXAMPLE 2
YOUR ACTION — What will you be doing for the people you are helping/designing for?	*Create a way...*	*Partner with...*
FOR WHO — Who are you actually designing for? (Not always the customer/end user.)	*the government...*	*large organisations...*
THEIR NEW ABILITY — What will they be able to do as a result of your work?	*can deliberately and meaningfully design...*	*help disrupt their value systems that drive decision-making...*
DESIRED OUTCOME — What will happen as a result of your work?	*a better way to protect people dealing with displacement.*	*to alter what it means to be in business, from profit making to value creation.*

TIP

AS YOUR WORK PROGRESSES YOU MIGHT FIND YOU LEARN SOMETHING THAT CHANGES YOUR INTENTION, AND THIS IS OK...

as long as there is a good reason for it, and it is still meeting the needs of those you are helping in the first place.

CREATING
CLARITY

While my husband and I were on a road trip, we created a framework. We called it a thinking framework, as it helped us get clarity about all the different aspects of our business. This framework is now seven years old and it keeps growing in its complexity and relevance.

There are many layers and applications to this very simple model. Always start with your purpose, to work out why you are doing what you are doing. This is a question you can ask at many different levels, from your personal purpose to the purpose of the work you are doing. The quality preserved at each level of abstraction of a purpose statement is its enduring nature—how enduring is this purpose?

You are probably more familiar with thinking about objectives rather than outcomes. The outcome is aligned to your purpose and, in human-centred work, it often describes something that enables *people*. For example, an objective might be to build affordable portable housing, but the outcome is that people are safer and healthier because they have shelter.

INTENTION BRINGS CLARITY

Another simple strength of the framework is that it keeps things connected. A sense of purpose brings clarity to the outcome, while a sense of approach brings clarity to the plan. They both enable you to articulate the intention behind your actions.

The thinking framework creates clarity between our purpose, outcome, approach and plan. It allows us to have a connected narrative about what we are doing and why.

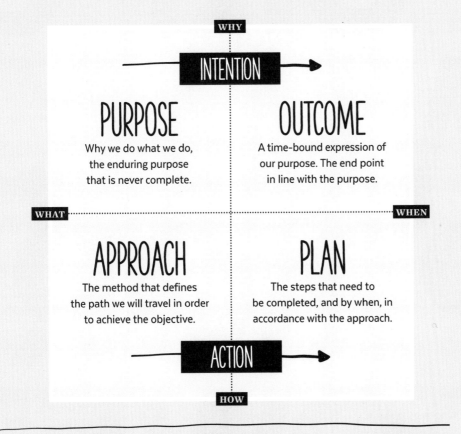

WHY

INTENTION

PURPOSE
Why we do what we do, the enduring purpose that is never complete.

OUTCOME
A time-bound expression of our purpose. The end point in line with the purpose.

WHAT

WHEN

APPROACH
The method that defines the path we will travel in order to achieve the objective.

PLAN
The steps that need to be completed, and by when, in accordance with the approach.

ACTION

HOW

HAVING A SENSE OF PURPOSE PROVIDES THE INTENTION FOR YOUR OUTCOMES AND YOUR SENSE OF DIRECTION.

TIP

THE INTENTION
To create a way for the government to deliberately and meaningfully design better ways of protecting people who are dealing with displacement.

THE PURPOSE
To improve the quality of life of people escaping danger in their troubled home nations.

THE OUTCOME
Displaced people are rapidly and successfully integrated into the community in a dignified and respectful way.

Let's look at this in relation to the intention statement we created earlier.

"PURPO
WITHO
PRIORI
POWER

SE
UT
TY IS
LESS."

Gary Keller

CLARITY AND FOCUS

At this stage of the design process, you are deliberately creating a world you know is possible. To do this, you need an incredible amount of clarity and focus. Your clarity comes from why you are doing what you are doing and your focus comes from what you need to do by when. This is shown in this simple thinking framework.

As your work progresses and you invite more people to interact with it, you need to process more perspectives. This can be quite distracting. Your clarity and focus will help you determine what is a distraction and what is essential.

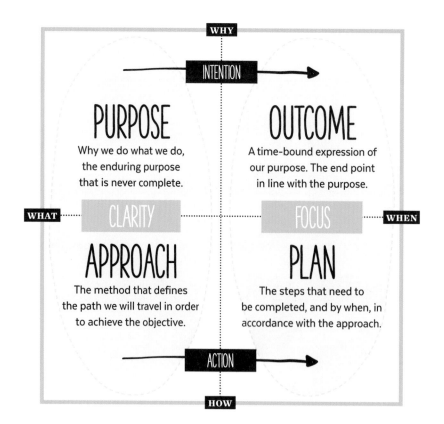

WHY

INTENTION

PURPOSE
Why we do what we do, the enduring purpose that is never complete.

OUTCOME
A time-bound expression of our purpose. The end point in line with the purpose.

WHAT CLARITY FOCUS **WHEN**

APPROACH
The method that defines the path we will travel in order to achieve the objective.

PLAN
The steps that need to be completed, and by when, in accordance with the approach.

ACTION

HOW

CLARITY AND FOCUS
Clarity comes from knowing why we are doing something and how. Focus comes from knowing what we are going to achieve and by when.

DEALING WITH DISTRACTIONS

Make it a part of your practice to ask these simple questions.
If any of the answers are 'no', you're dealing with a distraction.

QUESTION 1
WILL IT HELP US ACHIEVE OUR OUTCOME?

SOMETIMES SUGGESTIONS WILL BE RELEVANT TO THE DESIGN ITSELF BUT WON'T HELP ACHIEVE THE OUTCOME.

Example: Someone might suggest a new feature that has been made possible by new technology, such as virtual reality headsets. It might be possible, but it may not achieve the outcome of helping the visually impaired navigate a supermarket.

QUESTION 2
IS IT IN LINE WITH OUR PURPOSE?

A SUGGESTION MIGHT BE IN LINE WITH THE OUTCOME, BUT INCONGRUENT WITH THE PURPOSE.

Example: A suggestion might be to make back-end processes as efficient as possible to aid the rapid integration of displaced people into communities. However, more efficient processes might not improve people's quality of life if they are processed too quickly and placed in inappropriate accommodation.

QUESTION 3
DOES IT FIT WITH OUR APPROACH?

A SUGGESTION MIGHT BE IN LINE WITH THE PURPOSE AND THE OUTCOME, BUT MIGHT REQUIRE A COMPLETELY DIFFERENT APPROACH.

Example: A suggestion might be to follow a more traditional consulting model to create a government service that integrates displaced people into communities. This might achieve the outcome, and be in line with the purpose, though the approach might not be human-centred and iterative in its execution.

QUESTION 4
CAN WE DO IT IN THE TIME WE HAVE LEFT?

THIS IS THE MOST PRAGMATIC OF ALL QUESTIONS.

WHAT CAN BE ACHIEVED WITHIN THE TIME WITHOUT COMPROMISING YOUR INTENDED OUTCOME?

Example: There may be suggestions that are aligned with your purpose, outcome and approach but cannot be implemented in the remaining time. If this is the case, it might be worth asking the question a little differently and using your creative problem-solving skills. How might you alter the work so you can get this done in the time you have left?

Your energy and effort will *flow* where your

ENERGY *and* WILL

With well-formed ideas, you can become immersed in the details of the idea itself, focusing on its specific constraints and how you're going to deliver it. The conversation becomes more about what and how, rather than who and why. Your meaning is always held in who you are designing for and why you are doing it in the first place—to what end, for what impact, for what outcome?

Your energy will start to wane if you become bogged down in the details of the how and when and lose connection to the meaning of your work. Sometimes when you are busy delivering, it looks tedious and meaningless. Your daily routine may be to attend meeting after meeting with people who don't see the work the way you do, who are not driven to do impactful work, or who really don't understand the difference. This can be quite demotivating and you might feel like you've lost your way. Especially if doing meaningful work is directly tied to your personal values, which it often is.

You need to create a mechanism that allows you to pop up from these important details, and take another huge breath as you connect with the outcome and purpose, so you can deep dive and keep delivering. The very practice of doing this requires your *will*, as the details of the design can be captivating, time critical and all-consuming.

ATTENTION AND EFFORT

Your attention will be on what you're focusing on. This might sound very obvious, but we often aren't aware what we are focusing on. It might be something you find really interesting, it might be your research or it might be the actual design. This is fine if it's in line with the outcomes of your work, but sometimes you can get diverted by interesting insights that aren't directly relevant.

For example, we often see relationships between insights that lead to the creation of a framework that more deeply describes the inter-relationships of the human behaviours we have observed. We could spend a lot of time defining and describing that framework, but this doesn't directly address what the service or strategy ought to be for our client.

It is important to be disciplined about monitoring what is pulling your attention, but don't ignore those irrelevant interesting things either. You never know when they might come in handy.

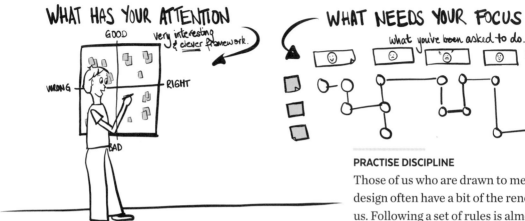

WHAT HAS YOUR ATTENTION

GOOD

Very interesting & clever framework.

WRONG ——— RIGHT

BAD

WHAT NEEDS YOUR FOCUS

What you've been asked to do.

TIP

BEING AWARE OF WHAT IS PULLING YOUR ATTENTION WILL HELP YOU ASSESS IF YOU ARE FOCUSING ON THE RIGHT THING.

Another thing to be aware of is how much energy an idea is using up. If there's something that is taking a lot of effort for you to sense make, group cohesively with other findings or explain its relevance, then perhaps you're manufacturing something that isn't actually there. Sometimes you desperately want to find something, because if you did it would be interesting to write and talk about. Sometimes you put too much effort into it and end up conjuring it into existence. Findings that are strong, resolved and real don't take a lot of effort to sense make.

At other times, we are so busy looking under couches and between the cracks in the bricks that we don't notice the Mona Lisa right in front of our noses. We excavate and explore bizarre associations when in fact the key insight is simple and clear, staring us right in the face. Sometimes when the insight is so simple, we think 'it can't be that' and keep looking. The key is to be mindful of how much energy things are taking.

PRACTISE DISCIPLINE

Those of us who are drawn to meaningful design often have a bit of the renegade in us. Following a set of rules is almost impossible. But applying discipline to your craft makes your creation more powerful: the discipline to keep going, to see the creative potential in all constraints, to return to the drawing board and keep coming back with the next idea and the next and the next. Just as an athlete trains to perform harder for longer, so must a designer who wants to change the world. Training your will and your personal power comes from practising discipline. If you say you're going for a run, do it. If you say you need a day off to visit museums and galleries, do it. If you say you're going to go to bed at 10 pm, do it. This is how you strengthen your will. You become proactive in the creation of your own reality so you can then facilitate this for others.

Without discipline, you'll be ineffective and, when you're someone who wants to achieve great things for humanity, this can be disheartening. Discipline is your friend... and remember, you can still break the rules. Discipline doesn't mean you need to conform with anything, except your own free will.

DOING WHAT IS NECESSARY

Dreaming, visualising and communicating an idea you are passionate about can be very motivating. But to bring something into reality you actually have to DO something. You have to sit down in front of your computer and finish the design, hire the developer, meet with the stakeholders, solve the problems, negotiate the constraints and so on. Sometimes you won't want to do that. This is where your strength of will and character come to the fore. It's also what sets you apart from the rest. Many people have dreams and visions and ideas they want to make real, but only a few of us are prepared to do what is needed to make this happen.

Doing what's necessary comes down to two things:

BELIEVING YOU CAN comes from your belief in yourself and your role in creating this new reality. Your belief is the essential ingredient to actually bring your idea into reality. Your belief gives you energy and creates motivation in others. People will look to you for guidance.

KNOWING YOU WILL is determined by your level of free will and your conviction about what you are doing. The greatest realities in life have been created by people who KNEW they were going to do what they said they would—no matter what it took. These are the people who make history and whose stories are told over and over. When you are creating designs for the improvement of humanity and you are faced with difficult constraints, you need to know you're going to get through it. You will make it through the trials and emerge stronger than ever.

BELIEVING YOU CAN + KNOWING YOU WILL.

"If nothing is random, and everything is predetermined, how can there be free will? The answer to that is simple.

NOTHING IS
PREDETERMINED;
IT IS DETERMINED,
OR WAS DETERMINED,
OR WILL BE DETERMINED."

Mark Helprin

PRACTISE RESILIENCE

Everything I've spoken about in this chapter can be summed up in one word: resilience. It can be discouraging when all you hear is, 'No, can't do it', 'It won't fly with the leadership', 'Nobody will want to use it', 'That would be illegal' or 'Can't it be a little more invisible?' Morale drops and you feel as if your back is against the wall. This is when your resilience is tested. You're lucky you are a member of the human species and we come equipped with free will. It will get you up in the morning and keep you going (because YOU said so), despite the feeling that you are being let down, turned down or rejected.

To be honest, if you don't experience this in your work, you're not pushing hard enough. I don't mean you're not pushing yourself hard enough. I mean you're not pushing the world hard enough. You're not challenging the systems and protocols and expectations and beliefs hard enough. If we are here to change things to be more sustainable, abundant and equitable for everyone, we need to give the current paradigm a decent shake up and create an alternative.

IT TAKES REAL GRIT
If we are going to re-wire the systems that contribute to the challenges that face humanity, we need resilience. We need to be Olympic Grade athletes at what we do. This takes commitment, determination and real grit.

CONFIDENCE *and* AUTHORITY

Who knew self-confidence played an important role in how you make sense of your work? Without self-confidence, you second-guess yourself, your ability as a practitioner, your findings and your designs. Believing in your ability to find a path through is essential to actually being able to do it. Without self-belief, your chances of creating what you have in mind are significantly limited.

OWN YOUR AUTHORITY

Giving yourself permission to have authority over your work is an important aspect to having meaningful impact. Sometimes what you are suggesting is new, and you don't have any evidence to show it has worked before. The following scenario will help you demonstrate your confidence in your work and foster your inner authority.

WHEN TO SEEK VALIDATION

You need confidence to avoid seeking validation of your synthesis too early. It fuels the energy you need to continue to wade through the data and endure the uncertainty and ambiguity your work evokes. External validation of your findings is, of course, essential to the robustness and reliability of the outcomes of your work, but knowing when to seek it can be tricky.

The uncertainty that an early validation introduces can be very damaging to nascent findings. I have seen ideas tossed away as irrelevant, only to be excavated later and incorporated back into the work. This is a very painful and messy process.

Seek validation only when you have fully integrated your work, regardless of what phase you're at and when you can communicate it clearly and in context. If something doesn't sound right to someone else, it doesn't mean the finding is invalid. It might just mean it hasn't been communicated holistically, or the person receiving the information doesn't have a reference point to make sense of it.

CAN YOU SHOW ME WHERE THIS HAS BEEN SUCCESSFUL BEFORE?

No, I can't. What we have found is unique to this group of people in this situation. And we need to design a bespoke service for that situation.

THIS IS TOO RISKY FOR US TO TRY. WE RELY ON PRIOR CASE STUDIES TO MANAGE OUR RISK.

I understand. There is always risk related to trying something new. Relying on case studies will always put you in second place, at best.

What we are proposing is less risky than continuing to do something that doesn't result in the outcome you need to remain viable.

We have worked with the people who will be using this service. They have participated in the research and the design of the concepts. We are as confident as we can be about trying something new with these people.

IF WE GO AHEAD WITH THIS, HOW MIGHT WE MITIGATE OUR RISK, GIVEN THAT IT HAS NEVER BEEN TRIED BEFORE?

We'll involve representatives of all the people involved in delivering the service from your organisation as well as the people who will be using the service.

We will be creating cheap prototypes and testing early. This prototyping approach is like your risk mitigation pathway. It allows you to see whether it is working in the market and whether your organisation can actually deliver upon the promise.

As we learn more we will integrate the learnings into the next iteration. This is a much more risk-averse approach than building something completely new and then going to market with a complete offering and hoping it succeeds.

TIP

AS DESIGNERS WE ARE USED TO BEING IN AN EMERGENT SPACE OF NOT REALLY KNOWING WHAT WE'RE GOING TO FIND NEXT.

This is a state of perpetual beginner's mind. Often this means we don't back ourselves when we see something out of the ordinary.

Creation requires *energy*. Your job is to harness it and *direct it*.

TO
sum UP

Creating something from nothing requires energy. Much of this energy has to come from you, and you'll need to learn how to manage this process. Sometimes you'll feel fantastic, and sometimes you'll feel depleted. Having a clear sense of intention, knowing why you're doing the work you're doing and believing in yourself are great sources of energy. Your free will summons this energy and your intention allows you to direct it. And remember—it's not all up to you. Your ability to connect with people will give you the support you need to work through the tough times.

NEXT...
Hard work doesn't mean not enjoying what you do. The next chapter explores how to inject your work with a sense of fun and passion.

EMOTION

Creating emotional resonance and connection
between your designs and people

6

WE NEED TO DESIGN FOR THE WHOLE HUMAN EXPERIENCE, THIS MEANS...

DESIGNING

MEANINGFUL

WITH   FOR

EMOTION

ALLOWS ACCESS TO

EMPATHY AND COMPASSION

BUILDS AN

EMOTIONAL CONNECTION

SO YOU CAN CREATE....

IMPACT

Functional design ensures we meet the task needs of those we are designing for.

THIS IS THE BASIC CRITERIA FOR DESIGN.

But your job as a human-centred designer is not simply to meet the minimum functional requirements of human existence, it is to create experiences that cater for the whole human experience. This is emotional design.

CHAPTER 6
This chapter explores how to design for and with emotion.

COMPASSION *and* DESIGN

The assumptions we make about other people's realities have been discussed often in this book. One example is our perception of how to help the millions of displaced people around the world. We assume theirs is a desperate situation so we may believe a purely functional solution is enough. It is not enough. We also need to consider their human-ity—their dignity, standards and values.

> '... *designing ethically is not just a matter of the appropriation and application of ethics but rather, and essentially, the designers becoming ethically constituted. Thereafter, being ethical and being a designer become indistinguishable.'—Tony Fry*

There is always room for compassion-ate design and the incorporation of that understanding into our creations. This doesn't mean that it takes longer or is more expensive, it just means we need to be considerate of the whole human experience in our designs.

DESIGNING *for* EMOTIONS

The importance of designing for emotions is made very clear in this fact:

MOST PEOPLE MOVE AWAY FROM PAIN AND TOWARDS PLEASURE.

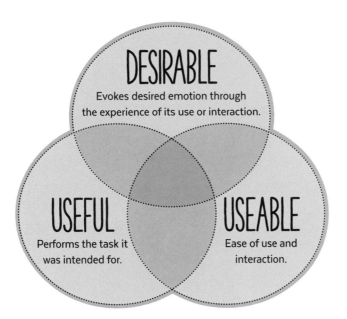

DESIRABLE
Evokes desired emotion through the experience of its use or interaction.

USEFUL
Performs the task it was intended for.

USEABLE
Ease of use and interaction.

Even human-centred designers sometimes forget to think about how our designs are going to make people feel when they are using them. We tend to focus on the functionality of what we are designing. We make sure those functions are present and designed in a way that addresses the needs and motivations uncovered in the research. Getting this right is often enough of a task, let alone thinking about how people will feel.

There are three fundamental features of a complete design for humans:

1. *The design performs the task it was created for.*
2. *The design is easily used or interacted with to perform that task.*
3. *The design evokes desired feelings from the experience of performing the task.*

These features have been summarised by Elizabeth B.–N. Sanders as 'useful', 'usable' and 'desirable'.

The useful and usable features of the design often get most of the attention. Does it complete the task? Can the person

We cannot forget emotions, as they drive desirability.

you designed for actually use it? Both these questions can be answered relatively objectively. The third feature relates to pleasure and aesthetics—it is here that we head into more subjective territory.

There is much more to the experience of life than successfully meeting basic needs. Humans are emotional beings. We embrace concepts like beauty, awe and wonder, which contribute to the connection we have with each other and our environment.

As practitioners who have the perspective, tools and intention to design a new reality for humanity, we need to pay attention to the emotional context and intention of our designs. You must maintain a focus on human emotional experience as well as the functional fulfilment of needs. Designing for emotions allows those who experience your design to feel a connection with your work. You will also form a deeper connection with the people you are working with, which gives your work longevity and increases the chances of impact.

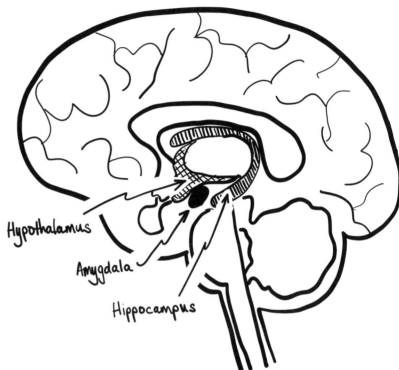

Hypothalamus

Amygdala

Hippocampus

EMOTIONS AREN'T EXPLICIT

It can be difficult to uncover the emotions associated with someone's experience of a product or service. Even when you've used an empathy map, sometimes

people still answer the 'feeling' questions functionally. For example, you might get a response like, 'I felt like it was taking too long' or 'I felt like there were too many choices'. These statements do not describe emotions.

There are good reasons why we find it difficult to name our feelings. It is partly because of our brain and partly because of society. Emotions are processed by the limbic system, within which sit the amygdala and hypothalamus. The amygdala is

WHERE YOUR EMOTIONS LIVE
Our emotions are processes deep within our brains. The signals get projected to our cortex before we can attribute language to them. Our body responds first, then the words come.

a small organ that assesses the emotional value of an event, mainly to do with aggression and fear. The hypothalamus regulates how to respond to that emotional event, and is connected to the nervous and endocrine systems.

Emotional stimulus is first felt in the body. Your heart begins to race and your stomach feels tight. This is your amygdala and hypothalamus doing their job. It is only when the amygdala sends signals to the language regions of your cortex that you can start assigning language to what you are experiencing. Sometimes it is easier to describe the symptom of the emotion—'I have a funny feeling in my stomach'—rather than the emotion itself.

We are not brought up to be emotionally fluent. Much of our emotional intelligence is learned in the playground. We are not explicitly taught how emotions are created in the body and how to map those feelings and sensations to words. When someone asks how we are feeling, the most common responses are 'good' or 'bad'. These are not descriptions of feelings. (As adults, we don't even respond with 'bad', because we don't want to make the other person feel awkward. Instead, we use nondescript phrases like 'not so good'.)

Because emotions are not easy for us to describe, they are difficult to access as input into your design. Understanding the emotional context for an individual may require you to use different methods to get insight. Just asking them how they would like to feel when they are using the service you are designing, for example, may get you a very superficial understanding.

To connect with a person's emotional context, you need to engage with them more personally. Asking them to describe how they are feeling about a particular experience will only tell what they can express in words, and only what they want you to hear. But when you observe them using the service, you will see what they actually do (such as workarounds). You can then discuss those actions in order to gain more insight into their actual experience.

If you ask them to make something, and add that you'd like them to express how they feel about the experience, their underlying feelings will be communicated through the artefact they create. Emotional artefacts can be things like drawings, collages and journals.

Looking for an emotional connection between yourself and the people you are designing for builds your empathy. It allows you to infuse your design with their desired experience, ensuring that you are designing for desirability, not just usefulness and usability.

This framework has been adapted from Dr Elizabeth B.-N. Sanders, originator of the 'of the Say, Do, Make' model.

DISCOVERING EMOTIONS

TECHNIQUE

SAY

Example: Workshops, focus groups.

DO

Example: Contextual enquiry, observational research.

MAKE

Example: Artefact creation, collage, journals, maps, diagrams, drawings, stories.

THINK & SAY

DO & USE

KNOW & FEEL

DREAM

TYPE OF INSIGHT

EXPLICIT KNOWLEDGE

Learning what people can express in words.

OBSERVATIONAL EXPERIENCE

Observing their behaviour and seeing things they don't realise they do.

TACIT KNOWLEDGE

Gaining insight into their perceptions of their experience and their feelings to build empathy.

LATENT NEEDS

Accessing what they dream of provides a future view and hints of latent needs.

TIP

WE NEED A COMBINATION OF APPROACHES TO CONNECT WITH THE EMOTIONAL CONTEXT OF OUR DESIGN.

UNDERSTANDING EMPATHY

Daniel Goleman, the author of *Emotional Intelligence*, describes three types of empathy: cognitive, emotional and compassionate. Knowing the type of empathy you are experiencing lets you watch for the different impacts that type of thinking may have.

People feel empathy in different ways. An emotionally sensitive person is more likely to experience emotional empathy than a person who is less so. It doesn't really matter if you are better at experiencing cognitive or emotional empathy.

What matters is that you know there is a difference and you can manage yourself accordingly.

As a human-centred designer, you do need to master compassionate empathy. You will have to design effectively and meaningfully in many different situations. Having too much of an emotional investment can be draining and cloud your perspective on the most appropriate design for that particular human context. Having too little may mean you miss the nuances that emotional empathy often communicates and reveals.

TIP

KNOWING THE THREE DIFFERENT TYPES OF EMPATHY HELPS YOU TO UNDERSTAND IF WHAT YOU ARE EXPERIENCING IS CONSTRUCTIVE OR DESTRUCTIVE FOR YOUR WORK.

COGNITIVE	EMOTIONAL	COMPASSIONATE

When you can see things from their perspective (also known as perspective taking).	When you actually feel what they feel (also known as emotional contagion).	When you can appreciate what they feel and can do something to support them.
Can result in an over-intellectualisation of your insight, leading to loss of meaning.	*Can result in transference, where you lose the benefit of being an external observer.*	*The balanced point of view that allows you to design with compassion and objectivity.*

"Compassion is not the same as empathy or altruism, though the concepts are related. While empathy refers more generally to our ability to take the perspective of and feel the emotions of another person, *compassion is when those feelings and thoughts include the desire to help.*"

Greater Good, University of California, Berkeley

RECOGNISING EMPATHY TYPES

Knowing how you are empathising helps ensure you don't get too involved emotionally, or stay too detached intellectually.

COGNITIVE EMPATHY

What did you do? How did you feel? If you are full of questions about the 'what' and 'how' of the event, you're heading towards cognitive empathy.

EMOTIONAL EMPATHY

If you are feeling terrible (or elated) for the person you are designing for and it is impacting upon or influencing your decision-making, you're heading towards emotional empathy.

COMPASSIONATE EMPATHY

If you can connect with how they are feeling and understand what you might be able to do to address their situation, you're heading towards compassionate empathy.

AIM TO MOVE PEOPLE

A lot of your work is about people believing in you as a practitioner and engaging in the narrative of your findings and recommendations as if it is their own. Be clear with them about how they can contribute to your work so they feel they are an important part of what is being achieved. Without passion and the willingness to create a pleasurable, desirable experience of fulfilling the work, people can quickly become disengaged and disheartened. This applies equally to you, your colleagues and collaborators, and your clients.

We have already discussed the importance of having a big vision for your work. To ensure that something worthwhile in line with your intention emerges from the creation process, you need to start big. It is the same when you are designing for emotional connection.

INTEND FOR YOUR WORK TO MOVE PEOPLE.

If you don't think about this as a possibility, you will end up designing solutions that get washed away with the masses. For your work to have a significant positive impact, you need to think about how to create something that will have deep resonance.

When people are moved emotionally, they are motivated to take action. Emotions like desire, enjoyment and passion are powerful sources of energy. Even in the darkest of places, you can move people so they have hope and see a way through to a better future. If your work inspires this type of connection between people, you can have a great impact in the world.

ALLOW YOURSELF TO BELIEVE YOU CAN.

As technology has enabled us to create quickly and efficiently, we have focused on functional completeness rather than beautiful artistry. Beauty stirs and evokes the heart. Beauty is a pathway to emotional connection. Don Norman, in his article 'Emotion and Design', discusses the role of aesthetic beauty in the complete design of products. He closes his article with the provocative statement, 'After all, attractive things work better'.

Beauty is not just aesthetically pleasing. Beauty exists in many dimensions, like simplicity and elegance. There is beauty in a simple solution to a complex problem, and there is beauty in something working so seamlessly it is practically invisible. The practice of beauty comes from the intention to create something truly special, of high quality, which will have lasting impact. It is worth your time and energy to infuse beauty into your work.

Beauty also creates forgiveness. When we really like something, we are more tolerant of its flaws. I am not suggesting that making something beautiful is a way to hide poor design decisions. What I am saying is that if you focus on getting the utility and usability of your design right, AND you design something beautiful, you will create a connection with your customer that is more forgiving and enduring. Emotional design is an opportunity to humanise your work.

We must embrace this duality if we are *authentic* to be in our practice.

EMBRACING DUALITY

In Chapter 1 we explored judgements, biases and beliefs. Awareness of these concepts requires an advanced level of self-awareness and presence and it is very important to practise these qualities.

I use the term 'meaningful design' often in this book. Meaningful design doesn't necessarily mean 'design for good'. Meaningful design means well considered and full of meaning for the people you are designing for. Whether or not those people are 'good' doesn't influence if something is meaningful for them or not.

You are completely within your rights to determine if your work is in line with your personal values or not. I actively encourage you to only do work that is congruent with your own values, because that is when you will be at your best. But don't make the mistake of thinking that what is meaningful for you is meaningful for others. There are two sides to every coin and multiple perspectives to every scenario.

DESIGNING FOR THE SHADOW SELF

In human-centred design, there is an undercurrent of understanding that we are doing our work with 'good' intentions. I agree with this, but we also need to be careful that we are not letting our good intentions hide the whole reality from us.

People have their own intentions that dictate their behaviours. Society deems some behaviours acceptable and others unacceptable. The perception of these behaviours changes with geographical location, cultural context, age, gender, religion, time (era) and timing (situational). 'Good' and 'bad' are arbitrary and definitely subjective.

If we are to design for the human experience, we need to design for the whole human experience, not just the side we think is 'good'. If we continue to repress a person's need to express themselves in ways that might not be socially acceptable, we won't build tolerant societies and people will release their frustrations in other ways.

THIS WILL DO THE TRICK! FUEL EFFICIENT AND RELIABLE.

"THE
A

ALTHOUGH OUR SHADOW SELF IS OFTEN HIDDEN, IT INFLUENCES OUR DECISIONS SILENTLY.

 TIP

I am currently living in Amsterdam. This city is known to be very tolerant of people expressing themselves in all their glory. It also has a low crime rate. I recently read that empty prisons are being shut down across the Netherlands. The main reasons for the falling crime rate and empty prison cells are relaxed drug laws, a focus on rehabilitation over punishment, and an electronic ankle-monitoring system that allows people to re-enter the workforce.

It is important to design for the totality of human experience. This includes envy, anger, rage, sexual lust, addiction, violence and voyeurism. Aniela Jaffe, a Jungian analyst, says the shadow self is the 'sum of all personal and collective psychic elements which, because of their incompatibility with the chosen conscious attitude, are denied expression in life'. So the shadow self is not necessarily comprised of negative traits.

For example, if you grew up being told you were good at science, your creativity might be in your shadow. A gang member may be rewarded for violence and deceit, so their compassion and honesty might be in their shadow.

As people who have chosen to design experiences for other people, we need to embrace this duality. Something that is great for one person is not going to be great for another. Only designing for positive experiences really only considers half the picture.

Our shadow self influences how we make sense of the world, so it also influences our decision-making. Your research must be concerned with understanding not just the 'norm', but also the counter scenario, or shadow scenario. The shadow scenario is not necessarily a design scenario. It serves more as a sense-making scenario, and the insight it offers your design.

SHADOW IS UNIVERSAL FEATURE OF THE HUMAN PSYCHE

for which we bear full responsibility to cope with as creatively as possible." *Stephen Diamond*

When creating a customer map, considering the shadow makes your thinking more holistic and inclusive, resulting in a more resilient (and pragmatic) design and a better outcome.

CONSIDERING THE SHADOW SCENARIO

This process informs your design from a different perspective. When you consider situations where individuals might be motivated to work against the outcome you are designing to create, you are able to address these situations specifically in your design.

STEP 1

CREATE A STANDARD CUSTOMER MAP

List the participants in an ideal scenario. They will be mostly collaborative and cooperative.

STEP 2

CREATE A SHADOW CUSTOMER MAP

Create a second map of participants, but this time consider the shadow scenario.

TIP OTHER MOTIVES, WHICH ARE IN THE SHADOW, HAVE BEEN OBSERVED IN HISTORY. THEY SHOULD EITHER BE CONSIDERED IN THE DESIGN OR DISMISSED WITH A CLEAR RATIONALE.

THE EXAMPLES USED HERE ARE ABOUT THE DEVELOPMENT OF A NEW SERVICE THAT AIMS TO IMPROVE THE COORDINATION AND DISTRIBUTION OF AID TO DISPLACED PEOPLE AROUND THE WORLD.

DONORS	AID RECIPIENTS
HOST COMMUNITIES	AID WORKER (ON THE GROUND)
AGENCY (COORDINATOR)	MILITARY PERSONNEL
TRANSPORT DRIVER	EXISTING COMMUNITY GROUPS
EMERGENCY RESPONSE WORKERS	SUPPLIERS
GOVERNMENT OFFICIALS (LOCAL, REGIONAL, NATIONAL)	
PRESS/MEDIA	POLICY MAKER

MANIPULATIVE DONORS	PERPETRATORS
DISINGENUOUS AID WORKER	RESISTANT HOST COMMUNITIES
TERRITORIAL RELIGIOUS LEADER	BAD PRESS/BIASED MEDIA
HOMELAND MILITARY PERSONNEL BLOCKING AID	
COMPETING POLITICAL AND COMMERCIAL MOTIVES	
CORRUPT GOVERNMENT OFFICIALS	
DUMPING (UNETHICAL SUPPLIERS)	

HARNESSING
your PASSION

We are so focused on making sure our design serves the needs of those we are designing for that we often forget to design for ourselves as well. We are humans too. Turn your thinking and skills towards creating your own reality that sets you up to produce the best work you possibly can. The pathway to accessing your best work is through your passion and desire.

PASSION

Your best work is done when you love what you do. When you are inspired and passionate, your energy soars and you attract other inspired people and ideas towards you. Some people believe their passion needs to be the subject matter they are designing for—the global refugee situation, or animal cruelty, or environmental harm. They have a cause. Being passionate can also be about the process of painting, or sculpting, or building bridges, or human-centred design. Your passion can be content neutral. This is equally powerful.

Finding your passion and engaging your desire in your work is a source of endless energy and a way to access your best work. As part of your practice of design, you need to know what you really love about what you do and remain connected with that. Working completely in your area of passion might be an unrealistic expectation, but you should bring as much of that enthusiasm, energy and connection to your work as possible.

We can sometimes fall into the trap of seeing our jobs as functional ways of getting paid for what we do. If this is the case, meaningful design becomes very difficult. Meaningful design is a channel for you to express yourself creatively and intellectually—perhaps even morally, ethically and politically as well. When your work is a channel of expression, you move closer to the natural state of artists.

Some artists have a conversation with their audience, like Hofesh Shechter and Banksy. They are passionate about what they do, and this energy feeds their imagination and creative approach to their choreography and art. They are in a dialogue with their audiences, who are free to take from the work whatever they want. That is the whole point.

As a meaningful designer, you will have formed a point of view through the course of your project. This is not your subjective judgement on what you are designing, it is more about the story you want to communicate. This should be present in your mind as you create experiences for the people who will be interacting with your work. This is your way of expressing your thoughts and your passions for assisting humanity at scale.

YOUR WORK IS YOUR CREATIVE EXPRESSION.

PLEASURE AND DESIRE

The word 'passion' is often used in the context of doing great work. 'Pleasure' and 'desire' are not used as often. Knowing what you want, what makes you come alive and what your passion is plays a crucial role in creating the life you want to live. Spend some time thinking about it. As the old saying goes, a plumber's tap is always leaky. You need to apply your skills to creating the realities for you to do your best work.

Design your work so that you enjoy doing it. Know your strengths and work with them as often as possible. Build on them by trying out new methods and tools until you become competent with those as well. Expand your strengths as much as possible, as often as possible. This introduces variety and interest into your work.

We often forget to deliberately inject pleasure and desire into our work. These are your seeds of motivation, your source of energy and drive, and food for your personal will. Loving what you do and having a good time while you do it helps you weather the storms and be resilient in the face of adversity.

CREATING AN INSPIRATION WALL

Designing at this level, you need to be conscious of your own passions and what moves and energises you. It's important to provide yourself with inspiration that feeds these passions. One way of doing this is by allocating a wall space that embodies your personal inspiration.

TIP

WHAT INSPIRES YOU MIGHT NOT HAVE ANYTHING TO DO WITH THE SUBJECT MATTER OF THE WORK YOU ARE DOING RIGHT NOW.

It might be photos of the person who inspired you to do this work, a picture of your next travel destination, a coveted award or the impact you want to see in the world.

Create a section of the wall that connects you back to why you do this work in the first place—what it is you are working towards.

Your job is to create experiences that cater for the *whole human* experience.

TO
sum UP

Designing with and for emotions makes your work more human. Emotional sensitivity and experience is just as important to design as functionality, but it is often overlooked.

Being aware of emotions doesn't just mean thinking about the people you are designing for. You are human too. Pleasure and desire should not be foreign concepts in the context of your work. When you experience positive emotions while you are working, you do better work. When you are passionate about the outcomes you are creating, you are more likely to see every project through to the end.

NEXT...
The next chapter explores how to deliver your project without compromising on quality or diluting its potential impact.

DELIVERY

Delivering with commitment, resilience, determination
and quality sets you apart from the rest

STRONG DELIVERY

YOUR IDEA CAN ONLY HAVE IMPACT IN...

REALITY

RELIES UPON YOUR

COMMITMENT + DETERMINATION + RESILIENCE

AND YOUR WORK BEING

CONTEXTUAL
COMPLETE
ROBUST
RESOLVED

PROTOTYPING
+
OBSERVATION

SO YOU NEED TO BE

CURIOUS
AWARE
PRESENT
FEARLESS

THIS HAPPENS THROUGH

Title: This Diagram Shows How to Be the Person Designing for Colour People

Condition: New

Location: A   Aisle 5   Bay 17   Shelf 2 Item 1483

Description:

Source: (red)

SKU: 23MA36002VWY

ASIN: 9063694601

Code: 9063694601

Employee:

23MA36002VWY

1483

1483

1483

1483

Delivery requires you to be action-oriented, grounded and resilient. Strong delivery ensures more of your work makes it out into the world where it can have an impact. This is the time when you bring your creation into a shared reality and people interact with it, use it, test it and sometimes even break it. This is the time for you to be open, humble, curious and strong. A time to lean into the challenges, limitations and constraints that will come at you thick and fast. A time to show resolve in

MAINTAINING THE INTEGRITY OF THE DESIGN AND ITS INTENTION FOR POSITIVE IMPACT.

CHAPTER 7
This chapter helps you get through the challenges of delivery by exploring what it takes to deliver strongly.

COMMITMENT *and* DETERMINATION

In delivery mode, remaining committed to the impact and outcome your work is intended to enable gives you the focus and clarity you need to get the job done. Your commitment to the process and the people you are working with and designing for is your pathway when things get difficult. And finally, your commitment to quality ensures your work will resonate, have the desired impact, and also be a creation you can be proud of. Delivery is all about commitment and determination—continuing until the job is done, really done.

COMMITMENT TO YOURSELF

During delivery you start to feel the pressure of a looming deadline. Sometimes you actually dread the project finishing, especially if you have loved the work. During this time, it's important to maintain a commitment to your own health and wellbeing. Don't get drawn into the late-night/early-morning cycle we all know far too well.

Your commitment goes beyond looking after yourself. It is a responsible stance to ensure your work is delivered to the highest level of quality you can manage.

CLARITY AND FOCUS

Knowing what you have to do and who is accountable for it is the most important thing in emergent practice. The actual tasks might change, and you might not always know what's next, but you must always know where you're headed.

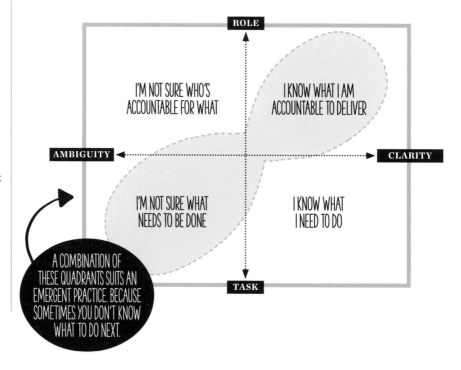

ROLE

I'M NOT SURE WHO'S ACCOUNTABLE FOR WHAT

I KNOW WHAT I AM ACCOUNTABLE TO DELIVER

AMBIGUITY

CLARITY

I'M NOT SURE WHAT NEEDS TO BE DONE

I KNOW WHAT I NEED TO DO

A COMBINATION OF THESE QUADRANTS SUITS AN EMERGENT PRACTICE. BECAUSE SOMETIMES YOU DON'T KNOW WHAT TO DO NEXT.

TASK

And that depends on how fit and 'with it' you are in these crucial final weeks. It also ensures you remain even-tempered and able to cope with the challenges that are going to come your way.

Ideally, if you've managed the scope and delivery of your work well, there won't be any need for late nights and early mornings, but I very rarely deliver anything without a few late nights towards the end. The point is to focus on maintaining your physical and mental wellbeing through this stressful phase. (I could write another book on this topic, but there is a whole section in the bookshop dedicated to this already. The important thing is that you actually do it.)

COMMITMENT TO YOUR TEAM

At this time, everyone is stressed and working hard. Your commitment to your team extends to making sure everyone knows what they are accountable for. The tasks you're completing may still have some ambiguity associated with them, but there should be complete clarity about who's got what.

ROLE CLARITY AND TASK AMBIGUITY GET THE JOB DONE IN AN EMERGENT PRACTICE.

ROLE AMBIGUITY AND TASK CLARITY RESULT IN CIRCLE WORK, AND DONUTS.

'Circle work' is when already-completed tasks are repeated by other well-meaning team members. It happens when people's roles are not clear. To clarify, a role is not the same as a job description. During delivery, everyone rolls up their sleeves and does everything they can to get the work over the line in good shape. There is no space to say, 'That isn't my job'. You might be a senior strategic designer, but your role might be to check for spelling mistakes because you happen to win every Spelling Bee contest you enter. You might be the project director, but your role is to keep the room in order and make sure everyone is eating and taking regular breaks because you naturally notice these things.

When roles are ambiguous, things get missed. Make sure you are committed to your team's ability to delivering strongly all the way to the end. Think about what they need. The visual designers might need content delivered in a way that makes their jobs easier, or maybe you just need to let them get on with doing their work. The worst thing you can do is hover when your team needs to deliver.

COMMITMENT TO PEOPLE

Be clear about the people in the chain between your work and its impact in the real world. Design for them too.

YOURSELF

Look after yourself so you can deliver well. Maintain commitment to your wellbeing, to ensure your work is delivered to the highest level of quality you can manage.

TEAM

Make sure your team knows how they can help and are clear on their role. There should be complete clarity about who's got what.

USER

Ensure what you and your team deliver is something your client can use easily. Remember who you are actually designing for.

EMPLOYEES

Ensure you support the user of your work to influence the employees responsible for the service you've designed.

CUSTOMER

Enable your insights to make it all the way through to the customer by also designing for the people in-between.

Be human-centred in everything you do.

COMMITMENT TO THE USER

I dislike the term 'user', but it can be useful to distinguish between the different people you work with in a project. The user is the person who receives your work and then does something with it. Remember who you are *actually* designing for. Make their job as easy as possible. Delivering work that is hard to decipher, not written in their language or is in an awkward format has a significantly negative impact on their perception of it. Your research, concepts and design can be brilliant, but if what you deliver is not useable, it doesn't really matter.

Human-centred design isn't just focused on the end customer, it is focused on everyone that your work will be (hopefully) influencing. Consider all of them.

COMMITMENT TO THE EMPLOYEES

This is particularly important in service design. Your design might be brilliant, answering all the needs and desires of the customers. But if it is impossible for the organisation to deliver, it won't make it.

It is essential that you are committed to the employees who will be selling, delivering, maintaining and supporting the service you've designed. It ensures your design is aligned with the organisation, and stands a chance of success.

During delivery, it is critical that you test your service design with the people who will be responsible for enacting it. Remember, you are designing for them too.

COMMITMENT TO THE CUSTOMER

And, of course, it is essential that your design is connected with the insights about who the customer is, what they need and how you can help them fulfil those needs. It is easy to focus intently on the customer as the main focus of your design. This is of course the case. It is crucial to remember who will be receiving the output of your work directly, they are YOUR customer and so you need to design for them too. What are their needs, wants and desires? How might your work address those?

COMMITMENT TO IMPACT

The urge to focus on the details of the 'object of design' as you deliver is strong. You can easily lose touch with the context and impact your designs are ultimately in service of. An easy way to reconnect with your desired impact is to pull out the system diagram you created in Chapter 2, when you were envisioning the possible outcomes of your work. The system diagram helps you connect with your big thinking and the impact scenarios help you connect with your original epic 'how might we...' questions, the context of your enquiry and the intended outcome. Testing your refined designs against these ensures you keep an impact dialogue alive in your mind as you tend to the details of delivery.

COMMITMENT TO QUALITY

It takes a commitment to every last detail to deliver a design of high quality and integrity that will stand the test of time and have the impact you intended. You have combined insight with inspiration, imagination and perspiration to create this new reality.

YOU MIGHT AS WELL MAKE IT BRILLIANT.

This is not the time to shy away from reviews and critiques—especially if they come from the people you are designing for.

Even when you can see the light at the end of the tunnel, when time is creeping up on you and when deadlines are looming, do not relax. Lean in, work harder towards the finish line, and push further with every iteration. Commit yourself fully to ensuring your creation will have a lasting impact.

COMPLETING CYCLES

When your design starts to become concrete, other people start interacting with it. This is mostly good but it can also be distracting. Your work practice needs to include integrity in completion. Everything you do during this phase of design needs to be done to completion. If a change has to be made, make it completely—a half-hearted effort won't do the trick. If you promise to complete a task by a certain time, do it. Building integrity with your word builds your own confidence that your work will survive the iterations and testing.

PERFECTIONISM

TIP YOU CAN KEEP HONING YOUR WORK UNTIL IT IS PERFECT, BUT THERE IS NO SUCH THING. LEARN TO LET GO.

As you learn more about your work and how it can be improved, you might become more and more obsessed with the detail. This is natural and appropriate, but it can trigger perfectionism in a practitioner who has high expectations of themselves. Having high standards is great, especially in meaningful design where integrity and clarity of values and purpose are so important. However, perfectionism can also be a thorn in your side. It can even prevent you from delivering on time... or actually delivering anything.

Perfectionism can be a blessing and a curse—be careful of its shadow side. It's important to learn how to let your design go. If you are putting lots of effort into small changes that only result in minor improvements, it's time to stop and say, 'We're DONE'.

A WELL-RESOLVED DESIGN

A well-resolved design is always a high-quality design. I learnt this when I worked as a design engineer at Ford, working closely with the industrial designers who were creating interiors for the next version of the Falcon. Although designing a car is very different to designing a human-centred organisation, that experience still informs what I look for in good design.

THERE ARE FOUR QUESTIONS TO ASK ABOUT YOUR WORK:

1. **IS IT CONTEXTUAL?** *Does your design have situational awareness built in? Is it aware of the context within which it must operate?*
2. **IS IT CONNECTED?** *Does the design exist in a vacuum? Is it considerate of all the connections, interfaces and alignments it needs to make?*
3. **IS IT CLEAR?** *Are all questions answered? Is the intention obvious?*
4. **IS IT COMPLETE?** *Is there anything left undone? Has everything we said we were going to do been done to highest possible level?*

EXERCISE 7.4

ATTRIBUTES OF A WELL-RESOLVED DESIGN

TIP

A WELL-RESOLVED DESIGN IS ALSO A HIGH-QUALITY ONE. ENSURING THESE ATTRIBUTES ARE THOUGHT THROUGH AND REPRESENTED IN YOUR DESIGN WILL HELP CREATE SOMETHING OF SUBSTANCE AND IMPACT.

CONTEXTUAL	CONNECTED	CLEAR	COMPLETE
Is your design situationally aware?	Have you designed for all relevant relationships?	Is the intention of the design clear?	Is your design complete down to the last detail?
Is it relevant to the context of its existence?	Have you considered the transitions (time, space, technology, process)?	Does it avoid unanswered questions and varied interpretations?	Can it be interrogated for usability, usefulness and desireability and rate strongly?
Have you considered its unique attributes and subtleties?	Have you considered the intersections and gaps?	Is it explicit without assumed knowledge?	Does it throughly answer the original enquiry with integrity?

"I SAID WHAT I MEANT, AND I MEANT WHAT I SAID."

Horton the Elephant, Dr Seuss

TESTING *and* PROTOTYPING

Delivery poses challenges of observation, sense making and ideation. As you test your design and see whether it is feasible for the people using it, you still have to observe, sense make and ideate. But the context of your enquiry has now changed, as has the intention. It is no longer focused on connecting with insight, it is focused on delivery.

OBSERVATION DURING PROTOTYPING

We create prototypes to test the integration of insights into a design that is the conduit for impact. Your work is the vehicle through which change will occur or people will experience something new. As you go through delivery, you need to test your design with the people who will be using it, to ensure you're going to enable the intended outcome.

There are many different types of prototypes and many books that describe the process and method in great detail. I won't repeat those here. But the intention of a prototype is not often made explicit, so this is what I will explore now.

TESTING ATTRIBUTES (IS IT USEFUL?)

When I worked in car manufacturing, we did attribute prototyping. Attributes are the qualities and requirements of a module. For example, a climate control system must be able to reduce the cabin temperature from a high temperature to a low temperature in a certain amount of time. This is a requirement and also a design standard. The engineers would create a rig of the car as accurately as possible so they could test this attribute with the modules they have in mind. Modules were taped together, hung from brackets and wired up for testing. The intention of the prototype was not to test functional performance, it was to understand whether the attribute made sense and if it was achievable. For example, reducing the temperature from 45°C to 10°C in two seconds might be very uncomfortable for the passengers and put unnecessary pressure on the engineers.

In your work as a human-centred designer, the closest things to attributes are design principles. These are the principles that inform your design of features, functions and experiences. *Testing your design principles early ensures that what is informing your design is correct and meaningful.* This step can be skipped at times. Sometimes design principles are created towards the end, and done for the benefit of the client, not our own work. But testing design principles early and actually applying them to your own work is an authentic way to see whether they actually make sense and result in a design which is meaningful.

TESTING FUNCTIONS (IS IT USEABLE?)

The intention of testing functions is to understand whether they make sense to the person using it and enable them to complete the intended task. The same basic principles apply to products, services and strategies. Functional testing is the most tangible form of testing and tends to be done most often. The features are described, the functions are tested and interacted with, and you determine if you've created something that successfully addresses previous frustrations.

TESTING EXPERIENCES (IS IT DESIRABLE?)

Testing the experiences evoked by your design relates more to ideas about emotional design than if the functions make sense and are easy to use. Functional testing usually takes centrestage because it's easier to determine if something works or not, and people are better at talking about functions than emotions. However, it is also very important to set up tests of the emotive experiences evoked by your design. This determines if your work is desirable or not.

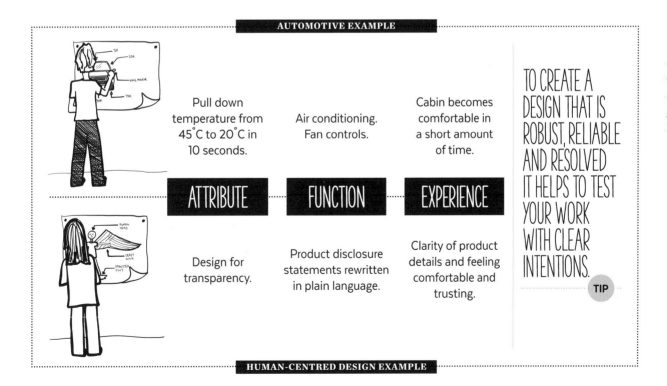

AUTOMOTIVE EXAMPLE

Pull down temperature from 45°C to 20°C in 10 seconds.

Air conditioning. Fan controls.

Cabin becomes comfortable in a short amount of time.

ATTRIBUTE　　**FUNCTION**　　**EXPERIENCE**

Design for transparency.

Product disclosure statements rewritten in plain language.

Clarity of product details and feeling comfortable and trusting.

TO CREATE A DESIGN THAT IS ROBUST, RELIABLE AND RESOLVED IT HELPS TO TEST YOUR WORK WITH CLEAR INTENTIONS.

TIP

HUMAN-CENTRED DESIGN EXAMPLE

Testing for emotive experiences is similar to exploring this during research. The difference is that you are evaluating your own design (e.g. a new service) rather than your client's (e.g. an incumbent service). You can apply exactly the same techniques to connect with the emotive experiences of those interacting with your design as you would in a research context, because prototyping is just another form of research.

As your design progresses, it becomes harder to test for these three dimensions independently. Your design principles become the informing criteria of your decisions, and the experience becomes linked with the functionality of your design. Dividing the process of testing into these three categories is meant to illustrate how they link back to the three dimensions you need to consider when you are designing for people. It enables you to bring a deliberate intention to your prototyping sessions and create something that is robust, reliable and resolved.

FOUR IMPORTANT STANCES

While the content in this section is directed towards delivery, it is equally appropriate for fieldwork during research. Often we don't consider prototyping to be a form of research, but I think we should. An eagerness to understand how people adapt their behaviour to a new reality during delivery will make it easier for you to make changes deliberately. There are four important stances to remember when observing the use of your prototype, or participating in any form of critique of your work.

BE CURIOUS

Being interested in what people think and say about your work requires a sense of humble curiosity. This is a stance of wondering why things are being perceived the way they are, and what sits behind the critique of your work. If you are testing your design in situ, you might see some curious uses of your work. View this with glee, not dismay.

BE AWARE

To follow your curiosity in interesting and meaningful ways, you need to be aware of your surroundings and be present to your context. This also means knowing the impact you are having on your environment and finding ways to make that impact appropriate. Remember that you will always impact what you are studying, just by virtue of wanting to observe or measure it. A sense of presence and awareness is critical to observing well.

BE PRESENT

Sometimes we confuse being aware with being present. Being aware is about situational awareness—the things that are happening *around* you. Being present is about understanding how you are in a certain situation—the things that are happening *inside* you. Be present during discussions about your design so that you don't seem defensive, disinterested or arrogant. By remaining present, you can observe other's engagement with your work objectively. This will give you a much better understanding of how to improve your work, which will result in a higher quality outcome.

BE DISTANT

Because we are in the most tangible state of the creation process, grounded in reality and in the physical plane, we need to keep a distance between what we are observing and recording and our own reactions to our observations.

As Hammersley and Atkinson point out, social and intellectual distance is required because it is in this space that the analytical work can happen. Without this space, the enquiry 'can be little more than the autobiographical account of a personal conversion'.

What they are calling a 'personal conversion' is the situation in which a researcher becomes affected and involved in what they are observing. They become emotionally connected with the people or attached to a certain outcome, and find themselves involved in the scenario themselves as opposed to being a distant and careful observer.

Creating some distance between you and your work will help you deal with critiques or change requests resulting from testing and reviews.

NOTICE THE DETAILS

Make sure you don't dismiss any of your observations as unimportant or irrelevant. There might be something very important behind a comment about your choice of typeface or why customers keep turning the product upside down or a mispronunciation of the name of the strategy. If you remain open and nonjudgemental, you'll uncover nuances that you can incorporate into your work, increasing your chances of creating a well-resolved design.

What you resist will persist.

ACCEPT CONSTRAINTS

As you bring your design into reality, you will be forced to deal with limitations and constraints. These may be in the form of opinion or legislation, or even nature herself.

A great designer accepts these constraints with grace, not resistance. This doesn't mean you capitulate and degrade the integrity of your design in accordance with the constraint. It means you see it as an interesting design challenge and find another way around the problem. This takes resilience and commitment.

The longer you keep going, the closer you get to making an impact. Just keep putting one foot in front of the other.

Sometimes constraints can seem negative at first and become miracles in the end. They prevent you from going down pathways that end up in disaster. Always be grateful for a constraint you know about—it's the ones you don't know about that can bite you. Prototyping is actually a risk-mitigation strategy. The more constraints you uncover in your process of design, the more you know about what's going to make your design a success and your impact worthwhile.

TIP

CONSTRAINTS ARE YOUR FRIEND. WORKING WITH THEM CAN BE CREATIVE AND FUN, AS LONG AS YOU TREAT THEM THAT WAY.

BELOW IS A STRAIGHTFORWARD METHOD FOR DEALING WITH CONSTRAINTS GRACEFULLY AND CREATIVELY.

STEP 1
SEE THE CONSTRAINT AS A NEED

Try to understand the underlying driver for the constraint:
- Why does this constraint exist?
- What is driving its necessity?

STEP 2
FRAME AS 'HOW MIGHT WE...?'

Once you know why the constraint exists, frame it as a 'how might we...?' question to bring a sense of possibility and generative thinking to tackling it.

STEP 3
USE GENERATIVE THINKING

Use the same generative techniques to come up with ways of addressing the constraints. Design is iterative and recursive. Just because you are in delivery doesn't mean the creative thinking time is over.

CONSTRAINT
The service cannot rely on us being able to give advice to the customer.

INSIGHT
Financial advice requires a different accreditation and your client's organisation doesn't have it.

HOW MIGHT WE
How might we provide clarity to customers without providing them with financial advice?

IDEAS
- Make information available to the customer that they can navigate themselves.
- Partner with accredited financial advisors.
- Become accredited to give advice.

BEING PRAGMATIC

Pragmatism means dealing with things sensibly and realistically in a way that is based on practical rather than theoretical considerations. Pragmatism in design is a tricky topic. Some people believe too much pragmatism can stifle creativity, while others believe not enough of it can result in designs that are out of touch with reality.

From a design and creativity perspective, reality is something created and designed deliberately and meaningfully. By definition, it can never be out of touch. However, a designed reality can be completely out of touch with the context within which it needs to operate. This is where pragmatism come in.

Knowing when to be pragmatic and when to dream is a dance that all designers learn as they become more experienced. There is no clear-cut rule. Just because you are in delivery mode, it doesn't mean you need to turn off the dream machine. Just because you're in concept mode, it doesn't mean you throw your pragmatism out the window. It takes time to understand when it needs to be dialled up and down. The most important point is that you need it. Pragmatism is something to cultivate and grow. It helps you 'land' your work in context so it can have impact.

SPEAKING BUSINESS

It would be a luxury to design in a vacuum. Imagine being able to create the ultimate solution without the worldly constraints of time and money! But this is not meaningful design. Meaningful design requires your creation to have meaning for everyone involved—the creators, the people who commission the work, those who receive the benefits of the work and the people you are ultimately designing for. Meaningful design not only requires you to be a good practitioner of human-centred design, you also have to understand the practicalities of business, operating a service, maintaining a service in operation, and supporting it and its users.

Pragmatism and creativity go hand in hand during delivery. Both need to be developed to create mastery in this field. Designers who care about the practicalities of what it will take to bring their creation into reality are more likely to create designs that have impact.